LATE-LIFE LOVE

Also by Connie Goldman

The Ageless Spirit:
Reflections on Living Life to the Fullest in Midlife and the Years Beyond

The Gifts of Caregiving:
Stories of Hardship, Hope, and Healing

Secrets of Becoming a Late Bloomer:
Extraordinary Ordinary People on the Art of Staying Creative, Alive, and
Aware in Mid-Life and Beyond
(with Richard Mahler)

Tending the Earth, Mending the Spirit:
The Healing Gifts of Gardening
(with Richard Mahler)

LATE-LIFE LOVE

*Romance and New Relationships
in Later Years*

CONNIE GOLDMAN

Fairview Press
Minneapolis

Published by Fairview Press, 2450 Riverside Avenue, Minneapolis, Minnesota 55454. Fairview Press is a division of Fairview Health Services, a community-focused health system, affiliated with the University of Minnesota, providing a complete range of services, from the prevention of illness and injury to care for the most complex medical conditions.

Library of Congress Cataloging-in-Publication Data
Late-life love : romance and new relationships in later years / Connie Goldman.
     p. cm.
ISBN-13: 978-1-57749-157-6 (alk. paper)
ISBN-10: 1-57749-157-2 (alk. paper)
1. Love in old age—Case studies. 2. Man-woman relationships—Case studies. 3. Couples—Case studies. 4. Older people—Psychology—Case studies. I. Title.
HQ1061.G642 2006
306.7084'6--dc22

                              2006017916

First Printing: October 2006

Printed in the United States of America
10 09 08 07 06   5 4 3 2 1

Cover: *Laurie Ingram*

For a free current catalog of Fairview Press titles, please call toll-free 1-800-544-8207. Or visit our Web site at www.fairviewpress.org.

CONTENTS

ACKNOWLEDGMENTS

Sincere thanks to those who inspired and encouraged the writing of this book. As my work led me to examine the many challenges and changes in mid-life and the later years, three books on the subject of elder love came to my attention: *Seasons of the Heart* by Zenith Henkin Gross, Edith and Jerrold Kemp's *Older Couples: New Couplings,* and *The New Love and Sex After 60* by Robert Butler, M.D. and his late wife, Myrna Lewis, Ph.D. I'm grateful for these writers' knowledge and interest in the subject, as well as for the inspiration they provided me.

Special thanks to the couples who generously shared their lives with me. A half dozen of my interviews were lost in an unfortunate mishap, and although these couples are not represented in this collection of conversations, their experiences informed me and allowed me to write a better book.

My sincere appreciation to my editor at Fairview Press, Lane Stiles. Thank you for taking my raw manuscript and shaping it up, and thank you, too, for your support in pursuing the subject of late-life love. Last, but certainly not least, I give a hug and a kiss to my partner, Ken, who gave me critical comments and needed corrections as well as love and support throughout the writing of this book.

INTRODUCTION

The world isn't made of atoms, it's made of stories.

These words from the poet Muriel Rukeyser have been a powerful influence on my work and my life. They have strongly influenced the shape of my career as a public radio producer, writer, and speaker. Like Rukeyser and others, I believe that we learn about ourselves from hearing and reading the stories of others. We gain insights and wisdom from people we don't personally know and may never meet. A story can touch the heart, bring a smile, or cause a tear. It can get a person to think, reflect, compare, or face a challenge or crisis in a different way. A story can inspire resolve, support a courageous stand, open the mind and the heart to a new experience, and ultimately change lives. Facts validate, but stories illuminate. This is why I've chosen to use the personal stories in this book to shine a light on late-life romance and new relationships.

Maybe you picked up this book to learn about the possibility of a new love relationship for an older adult you know—a friend whose husband recently left her or a relative whose wife has passed away. Perhaps you wonder whether older adults really can and do experience deep love and active sex with a new partner. Or maybe you are entering your later years and are feeling the need and desire to have a new love in your life.

Whatever the reason, the stories in this book will quickly affirm that love, intimacy, sex, and meaningful relationships are not the exclusive domain of the young. (How sad that in our youth-oriented culture things so obvious need continually to be affirmed.) For a long time I've talked with my aging contemporaries about their love relationships. In recent years these conversations have included many in new relationships. I've searched but haven't found any studies or statistics on the number of older people taking on a new partner in their later years. Yet recently I've been encountering such couples everywhere. In fact, my partner and I are one of those couples. Our story is in this book, along with those of twenty-one other couples.

Love, intimacy, sex, and meaningful relationships are not the exclusive domain of the young.

For over twenty-five years, my work has involved collecting and telling the stories of people in their seventies, eighties, and nineties. My efforts have been aimed at embracing the fullness of life in the later years, discovering who you are now that you're not who you were, experiencing the joys and responsibilities of grandparenting, exploring spiritual growth and aging, and dealing with attitudes of ageism in our society. Now my mission is to share the experiences of older persons who tell of their need for love, companionship, sharing of daily life, intimacy, touching, and sexual pleasure.

Late-life love comes with leftovers from other lives—adult children, grandchildren, health concerns, previous living situations, sexual expectations, financial discrepancies, divorce, caregiving experiences, grief and loss. Some couples have adult children who don't approve of their new relationship and refuse to acknowledge it. Others have joyfully integrated their two families. These are some of the areas we discussed in the context of new relationships in later life.

In this book I've chosen to focus on the World War II generation rather than the baby-boom generation. Many boomers are still raising children and building their careers. They have different concerns and priorities than retired widows, widowers, and older divorced individuals. Plus, there's already an abundance of information out there on "finding a new love in mid-life," "raising our children together," "dating again after forty," and "tips on finding the right man [or woman] this time around."

Despite the fact the baby boomers are now entering their sixties, our society continues to

Our society continues to perpetuate negative attitudes about older people.

perpetuate negative attitudes about older people. These stereotypes color our ideas about the abilities and desires of older people. I clearly remember a conversation that I had over sixty years ago with two other thirteen-year-old girls. We were at a slumber party, determined to stay up until dawn. As girls of that age often do, our conversations drifted onto the subject of sex. One of my friends said emphatically, "I don't like to think of my mom and dad in bed with each other and—*ish*—touching each other!" I reassured her: "Oh, I'm sure they're too old to have sex." Now I'm in my mid-seventies, many years older and considerably wiser. Yet I know that these generalizations persist, despite the lived experiences represented by the couples in this book.

Sol, eighty-one, who has been married to his wife, seventy-four, for seven years, shared with me his thoughts about the importance of physical intimacy in the later years: "Sexuality is a part of mature life. Some young people fear it ends at age thirty-five. They're wrong. Every aspect of intimacy is important—hand-holding and cuddling, as well as actual sex. It's an important dimension of life, and we joyfully partake in it." Bob, seventy-nine, and his partner, Meryl, who is seventy-eight, seconded Sol's comments: "People our age certainly have sexual relations in spite of the myth that old people don't do that anymore." Sharon, seventy-two, and Alex, seventy-nine, live in separate homes, but they share a good deal of time together. Alex told me, "We often spend nights at each other's homes. We have visitor's rights and visitor's privileges." Sharon added, "As younger people we each believed in waiting until marriage for sex. We were both faithful to our partners, and we believed that was right. We now believe that the commitment we have to this relationship, without marriage, allows for sexual intimacy."

"Intimacy ... is an important dimension of life, and we joyfully partake in it."

There are many ways to "do it," according to Louise, seventy-five, and James, seventy-two, who, like many of the couples I interviewed, spoke with surprising frankness about their sexual lives. "About fifteen or twenty years ago," James told me, "I became impotent. I told Louise about my situation, and she said, 'Hey, that's no problem,' and we proceeded to have wonderful sex. For me it was oral. For her it was manipulation. Sometimes it was oral sex for both of us." The stories in this book prove again and again that no matter how wrinkled, stooped, or aged a body may be, inside everyone is an ageless spirit—a desire to be physically touched and to touch another, to have some form of intimate relations, and to love and be loved.

In addition to sexuality, many of the older couples I interviewed are sharing their lives in ways that are less traditional than we might expect. For example, while some choose to marry, others choose to form less traditional partnerships. They may live together with no plans to marry. Or they may maintain a committed relationship while living in separate dwellings, cities, or even countries. What the neighbors might think of these relationships doesn't seem to bother these folks much. This may seem odd for a generation that grew up during a time when you didn't talk about sex, you didn't have sex before you were married, and you didn't live together unless you were married. Apparently, aging has loosened some of the social constraints these couples felt when they were younger.

Max, eighty, and Sadie, sixty-eight, told me that they loved each other and shared a deep commitment even though they were not married and didn't even intend to move in together. Speaking directly to Max, Sadie said, "I love you,

While some choose to marry, others choose to form less traditional partnerships.

and you love me, but we each have our own place, our own independent activities, and our own kids to spend time with. We live ten minutes apart. and if I need you, you're here. If you need me, I'm there. Why live together? This arrangement really works for us. We've had a relationship for six years now, and this is perfect. Many of my friends have found a partner and have set up a similar living arrangement. We can be with each other whenever we want, we have our own independence, and we both know we have somebody to rely on and be with who really cares."

An article in the *New York Times* recently observed, "Two decades after Woody Allen and Mia Farrow defied convention by living apart even after starting a family, researchers are seeing a surge in long-term, two-home relationships." The piece focused on couples of baby-boomer age, but the interviews I've collected of older couples reflect a similar trend.

Laura, seventy-five, has been with Robert, seventy-eight, for five years. "My dilemma was where to settle if I moved," said Laura. "There wasn't any space in Robert's house for my antique furniture or empty closets for my clothes. Our compromise was interesting. I bought a small condominium a five-minute drive from Robert's place, and we worked out a way to live together in two houses. Every week we choose what days and nights we'll pack up the milk, the bread, and the dog, and move temporarily into the other house for a few days. At other times, if one of us feels the need for alone time, we have a quiet retreat available at the other place."

I admit to being surprised by how liberal, open, and individualized these older couples were in their attitudes and lifestyles. A sense of freedom, justly earned, to make their own choices was evident in each conversation. Although not every couple stated it as bluntly, their actions reinforced

"Why would I, in my seventies, give a hoot about what people think?"

the attitude expressed by one woman: "Why would I, in my seventies, give a hoot about what people think?" Implicit in such a statement is the awareness that, although death may not be imminent, time is much more limited for these couples than it is for younger people entering new relationships. "Aging is really about the bitter and the better," one couple told me. Another expressed appreciation for simple things with the words, "Each new day is a blessing at our age." Whether married or not, the traditional marriage vow, "in sickness and in health, till death do us part," has a particular poignancy and urgency for these couples.

It's hard to know if the viewpoints expressed in this book reflect natural processes of aging, an increasing awareness of mortality, changing social conditions, or simple financial practicality. No doubt, all these factors play a role, though they work themselves out in unique and special ways in each relationship. And we can say with certainty that as the population continues to age, late-life relationships will continue to become more common.

For the sake of privacy, the couples in this book are identified only by first names, often not their actual names. But who each person is doesn't really matter. What matters is the truth of his or her story. Twenty-two conversations certainly don't say everything there is to say about this subject. But they do offer a glimpse of what seems to be a fast-growing reality: the re-mating of older individuals who are creating their own personal ways of growing a unique relationship together and sharing a late-life love. Older couples confirm the reality that, as a seventy-seven-year-old friend said to me the other day, "In the winter of our lives we can still find summer."

SALLY AND MIKE

I talked with Sally and Mike in the sunny living room of their condominium in the suburbs. Sally in seventy-one; Mike is seventy-six. Each has four grown children. Sally has ten grandchildren; Mike, four. They've been married for fifteen years. They met through a personal ad that she placed in a local newspaper.

SALLY: My first marriage lasted for almost thirty years. I've met and dated several men through ads I've placed or answered. I had been in a relationship for a couple of years with a man I knew wasn't appropriate for me. I decided to put one more ad in the personals, and that's how Mike and I met. I guess I was stretching it a little bit on my age in the ad. I was pretty close to sixty. I'm seventy-one now. Here's the ad:

> DWF—Divorced, White, Female. Bright, pretty, petite, dark-haired, mid-fifties. Healthy, interested in passionate life and love. Seeking warm, bright,

classy, emotionally and financially secure man to share life, fun, and romance.

MIKE: I had just about given up on establishing a new relationship, and getting married was the last thing in my life that I thought would ever happen. I had been married for almost thirty years and divorced for twenty. I have three children, now all in their forties. I don't know what made me respond to Sally's ad in the personals. I wasn't looking for a serious relationship. My cash balance was so limited that I wasn't even able to take anyone out to a decent dinner. This was the first and only time I ever did something like answering an ad. With no expectations, this is what I wrote:

Dear DWF: Your recent ad caught my attention for its style and directness. I will keep this note as brief and to the point as possible. I have been divorced for five years after many years of marriage. I'm well educated and have diverse interests ranging from intellectual to sports and the comic pages. I like to think I can carry on an intelligent conversation with most anyone on a wide range of subjects. I'm a passionate and compassionate man and believe I am fair, honest, and capable of deep feeling and emotion. I need to give affection and receive affection. I do hope you'll respond.

Getting married was the last thing in my life that I thought would ever happen.

SALLY: I had about given up on ads because I had kissed a lot of frogs. Mike's was actually the very last response I received. I showed his letter to a friend, and she said, "Don't throw this one away!" So I called him on the phone, and he said he'd come over and pick me up and we'd go have coffee. When I answered the door, I literally gasped. I could see he wasn't a frog! Even when I first saw Mike I guess I felt immediately that this was right. As he had said in his letter, he was quick and bright and funny, passionate and compassionate. It was a very nice beginning. We were the same religion, and I discovered that I had actually met his ex-wife at a singles event. I was seriously looking for a mate because I knew I'm the kind of person that needs a man in my life. I used to say that I was looking for my missing piece.

We actually married three months after we met. I had invited Mike to come and live with me, thinking we'd "try out" the relationship. He said, "Forget about that. If I give up my apartment and change my whole life, it's a life-long commitment. Either we get married, or I don't move in." I said okay. I guess I'm a little impulsive. I think we actually took that giant step of getting married without filling in the little steps. There were definitely times in those first couple of years when I had second thoughts. During those years, there were times when a little voice inside of me said, "Maybe you've made a mistake." When that voice spoke I always told Mike. I had learned over the years that when my little voice was talking and there was stuff going on, I had to communicate it because that was the only way it would disappear. Within two years the voice was gone completely and I knew this marriage was the best move I'd ever made in my life.

If I give up my apartment and change my whole life, it's a life-long commitment. Either we get married, or I don't move in.

For the most part I think our kids saw that we were happy, but one of Mike's sons interviewed me when I first met him. He actually interrogated me like a lawyer might do! "How do you think you're going to...? Exactly why would you after only three months...?" He kept trying to pin me down. Now after almost fifteen years of marriage, he's come around. My kids were pretty thrilled. I think that they really wanted me to marry again and find the right man. This was a fine, upstanding guy and he was very different from the man I had just broken up with, whom they knew wasn't right for me. So I think they really were very grateful that Mike had come into my life.

MIKE: As Sally told you, we were married in just a few months. I had some doubts those first couple of years. I knew I wasn't the kind of person that Sally was used to being with. I pictured her with men who were dapper, dressed nicely, rich and outgoing. It seemed to me that it was a different type of man that Sally would be attracted to. It took a couple of years for me to understand that wasn't necessarily true. I guess we did our getting to know each other after we were married. It might sound like our first two years of marriage weren't good. That's not true at all. They were very happy years. We were getting to know each other, and we really were very happy. But Sally had what she called a little voice inside of her that had doubts about the marriage.

I'm not self-conscious about my body with Sally.
I don't have any inhibitions whatsoever.

After a while I recognized that it was a very small voice, and I certainly could tell when it went away.

It was apparent when Sally and I first met that we had a physical attraction for one another and that has never left us, even after being married for fifteen years. I'm not self-conscious about my body with Sally. I don't have any inhibitions whatsoever. But I'm self-conscious in front of others. I don't even like to wear a bathing suit. I look at myself in the mirror and wonder what she sees in this body.

SALLY: I don't have any inhibitions with Mike. However, I still like to have sex in the dark because if I catch sight of my arms with all the skin hanging down, it's distracting. When I see it I think, "Who is this old lady?" I think Mike's body is great; I just don't like mine. I wonder what he sees in me. Mike is a very romantic person. He wasn't kidding in his ad when he said he was compassionate and passionate. We continue through the years to have a very romantic relationship, and I love that.

MIKE: You can see that our hands are hardly ever off each other. We're very physical. We like to touch. Right now as I'm reclining on the couch I'm leaning against Sally, and she's rubbing my leg. I'd say that for our age we have a pretty active sex life. We usually have sex in the morning. We're tired at night so we hardly ever make love then. We travel a lot, and these trips are always romantic settings for making love. We've been going to a place for ten years now on an island right off Puerto Rico. We just love it. We feel like it's our island.

In those early years of our marriage I recognized in Sally many of the traits and positive qualities that I'd never had in my previous marriage. Sally

> *We're very physical.*
> *We like to touch.*

and I seldom argued during those first years, and we hardly ever argue now. We're best friends and tell each other everything. We have mutual, complete, and total trust. I can't emphasize that enough. I not only love Sally, I like her. She's my best friend. She's always right there for me. I'm kind of moody, and Sally puts up with that. I can tell her everything, where in my previous marriage I had to keep my emotions to myself. I've now learned what good communication does for a marriage, or any kind of a relationship: spouse, child, parent. In my first marriage my former wife and I always kept everything inside, and I've learned not to do that anymore. I get tremendous support in my relationship with Sally. There's a depth of emotion that I never had before. Sally has taught me this. It's been one of the greatest lessons in my life.

SALLY: When Mike has been a little sullen for a few hours and comes to me and says, "Okay, I have to communicate," then we talk, and he realizes that holding something in is a bigger and more serious issue than talking it out. Very often Mike needs to talk about his alcoholic son. He's our major concern these days. In the early years of our marriage I thought of this as an annoyance and irritation. Now things are worse, and his son's behavior has become the background music for our marriage. Mike's son has been in treatment several times, has just gotten a third DWI, and is about to go to jail. We're both committed to saving this kid's life, and sharing this concern contributes to a very powerful relationship between us. This issue has probably made us closer than anything else in our lives. We walk a fine line between enabling Mike's son and supporting him. His son's life is at risk, and there's no right answer in this situation. Mike often says, "You know, were it not for that situation with my son, these would be the happiest days of my life."

There's a depth of emotion that I never had before. Sally has taught me this. It's been one of the greatest lessons in my life.

MIKE: I'm retired. Sally works and supports us. We both have inherited some money, so we have that, but Sally is the only one bringing in a regular paycheck. I have no guilt about her supporting me. I do a lot around the house, like the laundry and grocery shopping. I've been involved in the world of business for many years, and I'm able to give her advice from my experience. I'm totally supportive and interested in the work Sally does.

SALLY: I have my own business. My office is right downstairs in our house. The mission of the business is to help employers create a more flexible and supportive workplace, meeting their business needs but also helping employees meet their personal and family needs. We've just gotten a grant to do a statewide study of work champions in this "dual agenda" project. I love my work. It's exciting and fun. If left to my own devices, I would work all the time. I did when I was single. Mike has made me realize the need for a more balanced life. The irony is that my business is about balancing work and life! We now plan many weekends away and some longer trips as well. Yet, even going away on short weekends is very satisfying for us. It's important to both of us that we spend time together on vacations.

When Mike first retired, he took some courses in history and political science at a nearby community college. He loves to read. He's a serious book lover. I think Mike could read twenty-four hours a day. Then he had the idea that he'd get some kind of a job at the local library, but they wanted him for such peculiar hours that the job wouldn't work for us. So I said, "Why don't you just go to the library?" So now that's what Mike does. He goes to the library every day just like he has a job there. He packs a lunch and leaves the house somewhere between 8:00 and 8:30, and he's back around 4:30, and I put in a full day working in my home office while he's gone. Mike doesn't go to the library on Saturday or Sunday, but he sometimes reads at home on the weekends.

> *If left to my own devices, I would work all the time.... Mike has made me realize the need for a more balanced life.*

MIKE: I'm sure a lot of people would say, "What a waste of time to be reading all day every day." But I love to read and learn, and this is my time of life to do that. I like history, political science, and biography, and I also enjoy fiction. I'm actually doing on my own what has been promoted recently in groups and classes for people in retirement: "Late-Life Learning."

I used to be very active in athletics, but I don't do that anymore. Now I work out at a health club. We've had some tough times with our health. Sally has had bypass surgery, and I've had a slight heart attack. Five o'clock one morning I told Sally that I thought I had indigestion, but the doctor sent me right to the hospital, and I was there five days. I had a blocked artery, but my collateral arteries had taken over, so I didn't need an angioplasty. That was twelve years ago, and since then I keep nitro in my pocket but hardly ever use it. I don't have any other health problems except high cholesterol and high blood pressure, and they're both under control with medication. I'm careful what I eat and two days a week I fast, but sometimes on the weekends I binge.

We've had some tough times with our health. Sally has had bypass surgery, and I've had a slight heart attack.

SALLY: When we were first married, we played tennis together, but we quit because our backs started to hurt. The last time I played tennis I pulled a muscle in my leg, and it took me weeks to heal, so after that we decided to forget about tennis. Now I walk three or four times a week, and I work out on Nautilus machines and do weights. I've had two surgeries since we've been married. One was a cyst on my spine that was very painful. After the surgery I had a blood clot in my leg, and for several weeks I walked with a cane because my foot was partially paralyzed. The other surgery was for a heart bypass. I had been to the doctor for a physical and was pronounced "fit as a fiddle," but as I was leaving I mentioned that I had felt a little tightness in my chest while running. After a bunch of tests I ended up having a triple bypass. I'm doing fine now.

MIKE: Since Sally's episode, we think about things we didn't consider before. I think about how dramatically life could change. Every day I dread the idea of Sally passing away. I don't know what I would do. I think about my own death, too. I think about death a lot these days. My sister just passed away, Sally's business partner has recently died, and my brother, who is in a nursing home, has Parkinson's and Alzheimer's. I think he'd be better off if he were dead. Both of our parents are gone. You get to be this age, and you think about death.

SALLY: I know it's going to happen; we all die. Obviously we live in the midst of tragedies. They come into everyone's life. Yet I look at how life is for us right now, and I'm grateful for every day. Sometimes it makes me cry to think of how beautiful our life is. Over time I discovered that I was looking for a clone of myself rather than somebody who could give me what I really needed: a sense of security and safety. When I got into this marriage, I discovered a richness that has made my life totally serene. At our wedding, I said to Mike, "Being with you is like coming home for me." When we tell people our story it sounds like a fairy tale. We're so happy. We could be happy on a desert island. As long as there were some books.

> *I look at how life is for us right now, and I'm grateful for every day. Sometimes it makes me cry to think of how beautiful our life is.*

NICOLE AND TODD

Todd is eighty-two. Nicole just celebrated her eightieth birthday. They've been in a relationship for five years after meeting through an Internet site for singles. The couple lives separately. Todd has a large condo about ten minutes away from Nicole's elegantly furnished town house, where the following interview was held. I had not met Todd, but I had known Nicole many years earlier when she was married and raising her son and daughter. Before I could ask a question, Nicole eagerly began telling me the story of how she met Todd.

NICOLE: Two days after my husband died, a friend who always jokes and makes smart remarks, called me and said, "Well, are you dating yet?" There aren't very many people that would laugh at that under those circumstances, but the way she always joked about serious things made me smile, and I thought, "That won't ever be on my agenda." At that time I certainly wasn't at all interested in looking for a relationship, but about two years later, I had an experience that got me thinking about dating. I guess I was ready to see what possibilities were out there.

I teach writing, and three of my students won a national contest for older writers. There was an awards ceremony for the writers, and everyone stood and applauded me as their teacher. On the way home I thought, "If I only had someone to share this with. My late husband would have been so proud of me." It occurred to me that I needed somebody to love, and I needed somebody to love me.

TODD: I was divorced six years ago, and I immediately starting looking for a companion because I hate to be alone. I put ads in a column for people looking for partners, and over the years I dated a lot of women. I met maybe fifty or sixty women for coffee, dated some, but nothing materialized into a relationship. Then, in answer to one of my ads on an Internet site, I got an e-mail from Nicole. When we met for coffee, I was pleasantly surprised. Nicole is extremely attractive, much more so than the photo in the e-mail. So I asked her to have dinner, and we enjoyed each other's company. Nicole is bright and funny. It wasn't love at first sight, but we dated and got to know one another, and in about six months I knew Nicole was the one.

I needed somebody to love, and I needed somebody to love me.

NICOLE: But let me tell you about the other woman. You see, simultaneously, Todd was seeing someone else while he was dating me. So I told Todd that I'd give him two months to make up his mind—either me or her, but not both. When the choice was me, not her, my feelings for Todd began to deepen, and, yes, I can honestly say I've grown to love him. I remember telling my son, "I think this is it." Todd and I have a commitment to one another; however, we don't live together.

Both of us would rather maintain our independent living situations. I'm not sure it would go well for us if we were married or living together full time. I would consider getting married, but I know that wouldn't be Todd's choice of how to shape our relationship. I know things are better for him when he has his own place where he can spend some time alone.

TODD: I don't want to get married again. I've been married twice, and at this time of my life I love my freedom. This is the ideal relationship for me. I see Nicole three or four nights a week, we go places together, and we spend the night at her place. But I like my space. I like to spend time reading, and I like being alone some of the time. I think that's why my marriages didn't work for me. I don't like being with someone seven days a week. I guess I'm not the marrying kind.

I don't want to get married again…. At this time of my life I love my freedom. This is the ideal relationship for me.

I was living in a small, modest place, but on my eightieth birthday I decided to start living a different way. I wanted to live better, more luxuriously, in my remaining years. So two years ago I bought and moved into a large condominium. Nicole doesn't like to come to my place very often. She says I keep the temperature too warm and it's not comfortable for her, so she rarely stays overnight at my place. When we spend the night together we're at her house.

NICOLE: Yes, Todd comes over here most of the time. I'm more comfortable here. But I'm delighted he has his new place. Todd used to live in a very small, not well-furnished apartment. I'm happy to see he thinks more of himself and is now settled in a more appropriate place. But I'm just not comfortable there. I don't really know why, but I like being in my own house.

TODD: A lot of our differences are resolved by not living together. I'll give you an example. I've had some loud speakers for forty years. They're very, very large and have a wonderful sound quality. They're not very attractive, but I love them. Nicole hates the look of them. I said to her, "Why do you care? They're my speakers. It's my house." It's better we have two houses.

NICOLE: We've had some big arguments about how Todd should furnish the condominium He furnished his place modern, and I like traditional. But I went shopping with him at his request, and when I saw something I liked and felt it was beautifully designed I'd say, "Todd, buy this. It's a wonderful piece." And he'd scream, "Don't pressure me." We had some knock-down, drag-out fights over the furniture."

TODD: Nicole seems to feel that I know nothing about furnishing and that she knows everything. What she thought

A lot of our differences are resolved by not living together.

was beautiful and well designed, I just didn't like. It wasn't my taste. It was too feminine and lady-like. I have very definite taste. I know what I like. But Nicole has a controlling nature and wants me to respond to her choices. I get really angry when Nicole is so insistent about what I should buy to wear or have in my place. Maybe I'm more sensitive to that than other men, but I don't like it and I'm not shy about letting her know it.

I sometimes speak without thinking and get upset over little things and act like a jerk. When I get upset and start sweating the small stuff, I realize how foolish that is. I ask myself, "Why am I doing this?" I remind myself that at my age I should just get on with enjoying life and appreciating the time I have with Nicole. I have an ideal situation. I'm healthy. I enjoy being with Nicole. I constantly have to remind myself of this so I don't get distracted with little irritations.

Over the years Nicole has relaxed a great deal, and I have relaxed as well. That is why we're still together. We don't have issues over what movie to see, what restaurant to eat at, or things like that. But once in a while, the old habits come up.

When I stay overnight at Nicole's, I leave in the morning to do my things. I play tennis maybe four times a week, and I walk every day for about forty minutes. Mostly I do the active stuff in the morning. In the afternoon I work on my writing. I'm working on a novel that will be my third book. And I teach a class on comedy writing one day a week at a local college. And I'm an actor, so I wait for the phone to ring for a job. I've had parts in many television shows, and I do commercials, too. Evenings when Nicole and I aren't together I usually read. I need my time alone, and I enjoy it.

When I get upset and start sweating the small stuff, I realize how foolish that is…. At my age I should just get on with enjoying life and appreciating the time I have with Nicole.

Nicole's place is magnificent, and her housekeeping is fastidious. Everything is always neat. I'm not a slob, but I leave things all over at my place. I don't care that much about neatness, but it really matters to her. And we have different tastes in furniture and decorating as well as housekeeping. If we lived together full time, we would clash. The way Nicole and I have worked out our relationship is ideal for me. Marriage and living together could spoil it. But I truly love Nicole. I care deeply about her.

NICOLE: While Todd is doing his daily activities, I have my own things. I teach four classes a week on life history writing. I exercise, but I don't enjoy it, so I have a personal trainer, and that keeps me honest. I also volunteer for a large organization and serve on its board. I donate a good deal of my time to that group. I have many friends whom I enjoy spending time with. I see them regularly, and I have a weekly bridge game that I enjoy. I keep pretty busy. When Todd and I are together, we go to movies, the theater, out to dinner and to see friends. And we go on vacation trips as well.

We've negotiated an arrangement for how we pay for these things. We have a little box that we both regularly put money in, and that pays for our meals when we go out to eat. The funds cover some of the expense of our vacations as well. Todd and I share those expenses equally. I don't really like that arrangement, but we negotiated this and I agreed to it. I'm left over from a time when men paid for women. Todd is more able to assume the expenses, and although I can afford it, I feel he could and should be paying.

Todd and I share expenses equally. I don't really like that arrangement. I'm left over from a time when men paid for women.

TODD: Nicole can afford to pay her share. That isn't the issue. She just feels that a man should assume those expenses for meals and entertainment. And I feel otherwise. I think our arrangement is fair.

NICOLE: Taking on a new relationship in the later years is complicated in more ways than finances and living arrangements. You have to be either stupid or courageous. You know the reality is that something is going to happen to one or the other of us sometime in the future—illness, frailty, death. We're both in pretty good health and very active now, but we are in our eighties, so we can't ignore the inevitable.

I consider myself pretty healthy, but I had breast cancer fifteen years ago, and I always worry about the recurrence of that. I live with a chronic condition that causes my knees and my wrists to swell. It used to be helped by cortisone shots, but the last time the treatment didn't work. I'm going back to the doctor for further consultation this afternoon.

TODD: I do worry about sickness and one of us dying and the other being left alone, but I don't think about it a lot. Our life together is good and I want to enjoy every day. I don't have financial problems or the necessity to deal with career pressure. I have pensions and secured income. I can be much more relaxed and loving than at a different stage of life when I felt a lot of pressure. I feel completely free to do what I want and free to love Nicole. For us, a late-life relationship designed this way is great.

NICOLE: For me, physical intimacy is better than it has ever been in my whole life. Physical intimacy is a very important part of our relationship. We hug and kiss and touch a lot. When you have children you're busy and distracted and when you have babies, well the sexual drive goes right down the diapers! Now we might have less energy but we have more time. And Todd is really the love of my life.

Physical intimacy is a very important part of our relationship. We hug and kiss and touch a lot.

TODD: We're sexually active, and we enjoy it. I guess I don't have intercourse as often as when I was twenty-five. But it's better for me than it has ever been. I don't feel pressure to perform sexually so I'm more free and relaxed. And I love Nicole, so our intimate contact is wonderful.

NICOLE: There's a great difference between this late-love relationship and what my husband and I used to have. Some of that difference is because of children. When my son and daughter were growing up I often allowed them to cause conflict and chaos in the family, and it's totally different now. My adult children are very accepting of my relationship with Todd, and I think they're actually relieved that they don't have the responsibility of taking care of their mother, seeing that I get out, go places, and do things.

TODD: I don't have any children from either of my marriages. I must say that a bonus of being with Nicole is her children. They love me and I love them. I enjoy being with them and we have a lot in common and enjoy spending time with each other.

One of the advantages of being older is that you don't have illusions. When you're twenty you want to find the dream woman. Then when you're in the relationship or married you find out that there is no perfect person. Everyone has foibles and habits you don't understand, and most women don't look gorgeous when they wake up in the morning. If relationships aren't perfect it's easy to say, "I'm out!" I know about that, I've been divorced twice. When you're older, you see things differently. At my stage of life I realize we're different, and I've grown more patient and more tolerant. I know I have a limited time left, and I'm more understanding and accepting.

> *When you're older, you see things differently.... I've grown more patient and tolerant. I know I have a limited time left, and I'm more understanding and accepting.*

NICOLE: I think what Todd is saying is that when you're older your expectations are different. I often think to myself, if I had known what I know today about how to handle a committed relationship, I think I would have had a much better marriage. I see now that my expectations were not realistic. So I look upon my relationship with Todd as a second chance. You know, I think it's rare at my age and Todd's age to find someone to care for deeply. Some couples come together in a convenient relationship when they're friends and build a relationship on that basis, but I think Todd and I are very lucky to be deeply in love.

JUNE AND MELVIN

Soon after June turned eighty, she discussed with her five children her plan to sell the family home and move into a retirement community. She had been living there four years when Melvin relocated to the same retirement community after his wife's death. One day June was sitting in the main dining room when Melvin walked in and sat down at her table. "He told me his name, and I was speechless. I hadn't heard that name for many years," June told me. "We had known each other as teenagers." June is eighty-five now; Melvin is ninety. They originally had separate apartments. Now they're married and live together.

MELVIN: Let me give you a little bit of history. We grew up together. June's father was the choir director at the Baptist church we belonged to. Both of our mothers were members of the missionary society at the church, and June and I both attended young people's events. So we knew each other in our adolescent years.

But then we went our separate ways. I married a woman who played piano, organ, accordion, ukulele, and mandolin. We had the same spiritual background, and together we performed gospel music. We played for churches, missions, weddings, and retirement communities. We never charged for our music. We wanted to give our lives to the Lord through the music we played.

When I moved into this retirement community, I heard someone mention June's name. One day as I went into the dining room, I saw her sitting with some other ladies. I went up to her and said hello.

JUNE: And I said, "Who are you?" And when he told me, I stood up and gave him a big hug. Maybe that was the beginning of the romance.

I had been a widow for almost ten years. I wasn't looking for a man.

I had been a widow for almost ten years. I wasn't looking for a man. When I moved here, I thought it would be a good place to make friends, but I was thinking of friendship with women. I wasn't looking for a partner, so when Melvin asked me to go out with him, I refused. I didn't want to start dating at this stage of my life. But then he asked me again, and this time I accepted. It wasn't love at first sight, but as I got to know Melvin, it was really wonderful.

MELVIN: We really matched up so well. We both believed that, like the Bible tells us, God leads us and that He had brought us together. I missed my wife very much—missed the companionship and the closeness. But I wasn't actively out there looking for a woman.

JUNE: It all happened so fast that my family couldn't understand how I could become involved with Melvin so quickly.

MELVIN: They were concerned about finances. June's husband was a very successful businessman and left her very well off. Her family was worried that someone was after her money.

We became engaged quite soon after we met. I gave June a ring. We made a prenuptial agreement that each would manage his or her own finances. June's son manages her money for her. Money is the very least of our concerns. We both have a good deal of financial security.

JUNE: My son wasn't sure the relationship would last, so he didn't sell my apartment for several months—just in case. He wanted to be sure that we were sure!

MELVIN: Both of our families eventually saw that we were sincere and serious about the relationship, and we set a wedding date. Our wedding was right here in the main hall of the residence. We each had a one-bedroom apartment here, which we gave up for a single, larger place. We put our furniture together and moved in. Now we've been married over two years. This is our last move. We're happy here.

Our relationship is more than companionship. When we're together, ... we're always hugging and holding hands.

JUNE: Our relationship is more than companionship. When we're together, even here in our apartment, we're always hugging and holding hands.

MELVIN: I'll see June sitting in her chair maybe sleeping, and I'll go over and plant a kiss on her lips. We sleep in the same bed. There isn't such a thing as old age in our sexual relationship. Every night when we go to bed, we pray together. We have many blessings to be thankful for. I thank God for June and for bringing us together. And I thank God for all the pleasures we have together. We like to go to bed together and wake up together. God has joined us together, and we've become one flesh.

JUNE: I wonder if young people have as much fun and pleasure in bed as we do!

MELVIN: We don't really go out a lot anymore, although I still drive. I take June for her manicure. We go out to dinner sometimes with our children. Our religion is very important to both of us. When we eat our meals here in the dining room and we're sitting with others, I offer to say the blessing. We make it clear that we're not ashamed of being Christians.

JUNE: We've taken some trips since we've been together and enjoyed them, but I don't really want to travel anymore. We have plans for an Alaska cruise next summer, but we've decided not to plan as many trips as we did at first. It's so comfortable living here. I just like to be at home. We have all the conveniences we need or could ever want, and both of us have family living close by. And we have each other.

I wonder if young people have as much fun and pleasure in bed as we do!

We walk down the halls here arm in arm. It helps my balance. That has been bothering me some lately. I fell and hit my head on the piano and had to have three stitches. And one afternoon I fell in the bathroom. Now Melvin gets up with me at night and walks me to the bathroom. I had a heart attack six years ago but haven't been bothered with heart problems since. I wear hearing aids and so does Melvin. Melvin has diabetes, so his legs often swell. We take our vitamins, eat properly, exercise daily, and get a good night's sleep. I'm eighty-five; Melvin is ninety. For the most part, we have a wonderful life.

MELVIN: We both think of ourselves as pretty healthy. But if there should be sickness, I say that the Lord has given June to me and I'll take care of her. Who knows which one of us God will call home first. But I know we're committed to taking care of each other, right June?

JUNE: Yes, of course, we love each other.

MELVIN: We don't know what the future holds, but we know who holds the future.

CAROL AND MARVIN

Marvin and Carol are married, a second marriage for both. Marvin is eighty; Carol is sixty-seven. They quickly assured me that the thirteen years difference in their ages was not a problem. "Things like that don't matter at our stage of maturity," Marvin told me. And at their stage of activity, I might add. They are both actively committed to community and national projects that help older adults. Their financial situation allows them to live well, travel all over the world, and generously support the causes they believe in. When I asked them to tell me about their relationship, Carol said, "Neither of us was looking for a partner, but we were so lucky to find each other."

CAROL: I used to be the director of a local senior center. At one point I was restructuring my board of directors. Marvin came in with his wife and her father, who was ninety-five, looking for something he could involve himself in. I was very impressed with Marvin. He had lived in the community for many years and was a strong supporter of community programs. I could also tell that he was a very caring person by the way he treated his father-in-law and the way he talked about older people. Very frankly, we needed somebody on the board who had contacts with money people, and Marvin belonged to a country club. He was a businessman, and we needed that kind of expertise on our board as well.

So Marvin's father-in-law joined the senior center, Marvin joined the board, and several years later Marvin's wife died suddenly and unexpectedly. A mutual friend on the board said, "Carol, you're single and I think you and Marvin would make a good match." I told her I wasn't at all interested, that I was very happy being by myself. But this friend wouldn't quit. She kept pushing me to get together with Marvin. So I decided to ask Marvin to lunch to discuss some senior center projects. It was easy to do that. It wasn't like dating.

In the years I had been divorced, I had gone out on only one or two dates. I really wasn't interested. But with Marvin, I became like a young girl again.

We met for lunch, and in our conversation Marvin joked with me about how many women had tried to date him since his wife died. He called the women "the brisket brigade" because they always volunteered to bring dinner over for him. He said he hadn't dated in over forty years, and I jokingly said, "Well, consider this your first date." I really felt an attraction to him, both his physicality— he was a big, strong man—and his enthusiasm about life, even though he had just lost a wife he loved very much.

In the years I had been divorced, I had gone out on only one or two dates. I really wasn't interested. But with Marvin, I became like a young girl again. There was a tremendous physical attraction between us. He was determined to go on living, and he had told his children that.

MARVIN: My wife and I always discussed everything. I had done some very extensive estate planning, and in the course of doing that we also discussed what might happen if one of us died. We both agreed we'd go on living—whatever that meant. When my whole family was together after her death, I told my children that I was open to finding another lady to share the rest of my life. Almost immediately after the funeral I got about thirty phone calls from friends suggesting various women I might date. I wasn't ready for that. Instead, I picked myself up and went to Europe.

I thought about what I wanted in a new partner, and I made a list. I wanted someone who was family oriented, who loved to travel, who was smart and interesting, articulate, aware, down-to-earth, undemanding, sexy, attractive, and loved to be touched.

My wife and I ... discussed what might happen if one of us died. We both agreed we'd go on living—whatever that meant.

When I came back, a good friend of mine, also on the board of the senior center, told me that Carol was divorced and strongly suggested I date her. At the lunch that Carol just told you about, I remember thinking, "Why should I date thirty women trying to figure out who I wanted to be with?" Here was a very nice, smart lady. I really felt a physical attraction to her, so I simply narrowed it down.

CAROL: I knew right away that Marvin was the person for me. I had no doubt. I was afraid that I was falling head over heels in love and that I was being too impetuous.

MARVIN: We decided to live together just six months after my wife died. Her family was very happy for her, and my three sons accepted it comfortably, perhaps because I'd told them that their mother and I had discussed finding another partner if one preceded the other in death.

CAROL: I moved into Marvin's house. There I was, living in a place that his wife had decorated to her taste, and there were several pictures of Marvin and his wife on the wall in our bedroom. But it was only six months after her death, and he was really still in a mourning period. He would sometimes wake up crying. Often during the night he'd call out her name. I absolutely understood what he was going through, and I was glad I was there to comfort him.

My friends cautioned me that every man has a "transitional" woman and that our relationship would last only until he found the right woman. But that didn't happen because I was the right woman! I wanted to get married, and Marvin did as well. For us it was a tradition that was meaningful. We wanted that bond. Marriage isn't the way for every late-life couple, but for us it was what we wanted to do.

My friends cautioned me that every man has a "transitional" woman and that our relationship would last only until he found the right woman. But that didn't happen because I was the right woman!

MARVIN: I would not have lived indefinitely with Carol without getting married. That was the way I was brought up. But I didn't want to rush it. I wanted to be sure we were compatible, that we traveled well together, that we met and enjoyed each other's friends, that our children were comfortable with us being together, and that it really was the right decision for both of us.

CAROL: I wanted to take my time, too. I had been in a marriage for thirty years. I kept trying to make it work, but the marriage wasn't a good one. It was only when our grown children told us they didn't understand why we stayed together when neither of us was happy that I was able to separate. I knew what I wanted in a relationship, but I had to get to know Marvin in all kinds of circumstances before I felt I could marry him.

MARVIN: I wanted Carol to tell the truth about everything, and I would do the same, even about the little things. It isn't good for a relationship to keep a lie going, even a little one. In a successful marriage, there can be no skeletons in the closet.

CAROL: I've worked all my life, and I was working when I met Marvin. But Marvin was retired, and he wanted his partner to be free to travel and do things with him. So I had a decision to make about whether to retire as well. I wasn't ready to leave my job at the senior center. I liked being independent and having my own money and the responsibility of my work. But I realized that we would have a finite time together. I really wanted to be with him as much as possible, so I made the decision to stop working. I quit my job and volunteered to be the president of the board of directors at the senior center. Marvin says I'm really doing just as much work but not getting paid!

I knew what I wanted in a relationship, but I had to get to know Marvin in all kinds of circumstances before I felt I could marry him.

We love being with each other, but we did have a difficult transition period. One of our issues was the house. I sold mine and moved into Marvin's, then realized I was living in his wife's house. It wasn't mine. So we redecorated the house to my style and taste, and that made it more comfortable for me. Also, there was some friction over what Marvin expected. His wife had accommodated his every need. I had to learn to speak up and tell him what I needed.

One interesting thing that has happened is that Marvin has become involved in my field of work: aging. He had looked around for something to do after retirement and hadn't found anything he was excited about. I introduced him to several of my contacts in the world of aging services, and he took the ball and ran with it. We have that in common now. It has made our marriage even stronger.

MARVIN: I've become very interested in the field of aging. In a world where the old are beginning to outnumber the young, I like to work with groups and organizations that help older adults. At the moment, I'm using my expertise in business to help a large organization in my city distribute food to needy elders—through Meals on Wheels, to the homebound, at senior centers. I've worked three years now on planning, contracting, and financing the program, and the experience has been extremely rewarding.

CAROL: Between us we have six children and twelve grandchildren. We're taking each grandchild to Europe as they reach the age of eleven or twelve. We're comfortable financially, and that makes decisions like this easy. We know where our limits are, but we have pretty wide parameters.

[Marvin's] wife had accommodated his every need. I had to learn to speak up and tell him what I needed.

MARVIN: I have always had the philosophy of using money to make life more comfortable and more enjoyable. Carol and I agreed very early in our relationship that we would work at integrating our two families. The first thing we did to promote this plan was to take a place at the beach for a month and invite all the children and grandchildren so they could get to know one another. We've done this in various other locations as well. Carol has become friendly with my first wife's brother and sister and the cousins. And my brothers love Carol as much as they did my wife of forty-five years.

CAROL: Right from the beginning we worked very hard to meld the two families. They get together on holidays, and they consider each other one family. It was a planned effort, and Marvin and I are now very close to each other's children and their families.

MARVIN: The prime objective in this effort was to make everyone comfortable. It's wonderful to have such a big family, and we wanted to establish good relations with them all. I don't know what the future will bring. I see that as I get older my energy is less and my desire to travel has diminished. But don't misunderstand. I'm very active and have a good deal of energy—for my volunteer work and for Carol.

We have some kind of sexual activity three or four times a week. I don't have the greatest body, but to him my body is beautiful and that makes me feel wonderful.

CAROL: Marvin and I are very sexually connected. We have some kind of sexual activity three or four times a week. I don't have the greatest body, but to him my body is beautiful and that makes me feel wonderful. It amazes me that he can look at my body and think that, but he does. He thinks I'm the sexiest thing in the world! And he tells me all the time how great I look, how much he loves me, and how proud he is of me. He tells me things like that every single day. And I feel the same way about him. That's a recipe for success in a relationship!

MARVIN: If I were to use one word to describe our intimacy, I'd use the word "hugging." Maybe it's our personalities or our particular needs, but we snuggle all night. We touch each other, hold each other. Sometimes it leads to sexual pleasure, sometimes it doesn't. Carol makes me comfortable. The satisfaction we take in our physical relationship is remarkable.

You know, when I was running a large company with a lot of employees I was immersed in my work, and it colored my whole life, especially the sexual part of my life. Sometimes I just couldn't get out of my own way emotionally or mentally, I was so preoccupied with work concerns. Even after I retired I dreamed about work. I didn't have the responsibility any longer, but I would dream of business problems. I still occasionally dream about various problems of selling, shipping, production, administration. But Carol makes it easy for me to relax and let go of most of that.

CAROL: We don't argue often. But every once an a while when Marvin and I have a problem with our families or between ourselves, we'll meet with the therapist or we'll talk with our rabbi or we'll do whatever is appropriate to heal the problem. That's the bottom line, because we don't want anything to get in the way of our relationship.

We touch each other, hold each other. Sometimes it leads to sexual pleasure, sometimes it doesn't.... The satisfaction we take in our physical relationship is remarkable.

MARVIN: We love our life together, and I'm not going to do anything that would jeopardize that. I had plans to go on a fishing trip. The goal of the trip was to catch a 200- to 500-pound fish. I told my doctor about my plans, and he said, "Don't go. Your heart may not be able to take that kind of physical exertion." I realized that I was playing Russian roulette with my life over a fish, so I cancelled the trip. It all goes back to a simple principle; if I take care of myself, I can take care of Carol. I now fish for much smaller fish.

CAROL: Our primary concern at this time of our lives is tending to our relationship. We're loving and involved with our families, but we try to protect ourselves and each other from getting pulled into situations with our kids.

MARVIN: We've discovered that when we get overly involved in our kids' problems that I'm irritated, Carol's irritated, and nothing gets resolved. The kids end up doing what they're going to do anyway. Carol and I work very hard to protect our relationship from these kinds of family situations. We can't solve their problems. We've learned to let go of these kinds of things.

I try to make things easy for Carol, and she does the same for me. We have a big social life and a multitude of friends. We've met couples on trips we've taken, and we continue to get together with them. We have many friends. We've blended everybody. It's beyond wonderful. The rewards of spending the last years of my life with Carol have already been many. Our relationship is exactly what I want, and the best is yet to come.

The rewards of spending the last years of my life with Carol have already been many. Our relationship is exactly what I want, and the best is yet to come.

CAROL: That much-quoted phrase is true: "Grow old with me, the best is yet to be."

PAT AND JOHN

John retired over a decade ago after a long career as a chemical engineer. He's eighty now, and has been married to Pat for two years. Before marrying Pat, John was married to her cousin, so Pat and John have known each other for nearly sixty years. Pat is completing a Ph.D. For eleven years she has led grief groups and done presentations on death and dying. Pat celebrated her seventy-fifth birthday this week.

JOHN: I was lonely, no doubt about that. I noticed that my neighbors who had no companion, significant other, or spouse were rather depressed, withdrawn—in kind of sad shape. My wife and I had talked about what we would do when one of us passed away, and we agreed that we would be happier if we sought out a new relationship. For me, companionship is almost a necessity. But I wasn't actively looking for a relationship at the time; it just happened.

PAT: When my cousin—who was John's wife—died, I told him I'd come to the city they lived in for the funeral. I was the last of the relatives in his wife's family in her generation. Her sister resides in a nursing home here in the city where I live. She can't speak or hear, and is confined to a wheelchair. I took on the responsibility of telling her of her sister's death. I wanted something visual to help her understand. I made a photo album of pictures of her relatives that I had taken at the wake to use as a way to tell her about the death of her sister.

After the funeral, John started calling me fairly regularly to talk. I told John that I was a grief counselor, not a therapist, and made him promise that if it was something I couldn't help with or handle, that he would go to a therapist. John also wanted to talk about the trauma of being in World War II and other experiences he'd never discussed with anyone. That was probably the first time there was a transition in our conversations from just the bereavement talk of his wife's death. I was interested in befriending John, but I didn't have any other agenda. It kind of grew from there.

For me, companionship is almost a necessity. But I wasn't actively looking for a relationship at the time; it just happened.

John had qualities that were important to me: honesty, stability, and the ability to communicate. I realized, too, that we had a common bond around our interest in higher education and continued learning. In my work, I give presentations on the subject of death and dying. I'm also back at the University to get a Ph.D. degree. To be in my life you don't have to be knowledgeable about my work, but you do have to be okay with me being busy and to support what I'm doing.

Shortly after we started talking on the phone regularly, I found out that I had to have mastoid surgery. John said that he would come to where I lived and take care of me, assuring me that he'd had plenty of practice being the caregiver of my cousin, his wife. I didn't know how that was going to play out, but I was very appreciative of the offer. No one else volunteered to do this for me. It was the middle of winter, and he flew in a few days ahead of my surgery so he wouldn't be held up in an airport by a storm.

JOHN: When you take care of a person, you learn a lot about them. These times can be the roughest. We spent that week together, had long conversations, and really got to know each other. Before I left to fly back home, I told Pat that I was interested in pursuing a relationship. She didn't take me seriously. When I left, the last thing I told her was that she didn't appreciate the level of my determination.

I really enjoyed getting to know Pat, but I also felt I owed Pat's family something. My wife—her cousin—had helped me get my Ph.D. That really takes a team. So, to pay the family back, I thought, here's a graduate student that could use support. Why don't I offer to help her? That's when I decided to start coming to visit Pat regularly.

I had been married for fifty-four years. I'll always carry those years with me. But I knew I had to move on.

I had been married for fifty-four years. I'll always carry those years with me. But I knew I had to move on. When Pat and I decided we were going to stay together, I told my four children. One daughter objected to us being together. She didn't like Pat at first, but now I think Pat has more communication with her than I do, and everything is really fine between them. My son was concerned about Pat taking the place of his mother. He was still grieving that loss when we announced that we planned to marry. By the time of our wedding, my son had worked through his grief, and everything was pretty well straightened out and comfortable with all four of my children.

PAT: Overall I think my children were okay with my marriage to John. My children hadn't recently lost a parent like John's children had, and that makes a difference. John and his wife had talked with each other about having another partner if one of them were to die. But they didn't discuss this with their kids. Maybe if they had, John's kids might have been more comfortable about our getting together.

John decided that he would leave his house and move into mine. He likes the city I live in, and his house was forty years old. Mine is a lot newer. We had the same style of furniture, so his furniture looked perfect in my house. When John was getting ready to move, he had to decide what he was going to bring with him and what he was going to give to his children. I was very impressed with how respectfully and equitably John's daughters divided things up with all of the family. They made sure that the two children who weren't there got things that were important to them— Grandma's dishes and other things. They were very thoughtful, considerate, and generous to the other children who couldn't be there.

John and his wife had talked with each other about having another partner if one of them were to die. But they didn't discuss this with their kids. Maybe if they had, John's kids might have been more comfortable about our getting together.

John and I have been married just over two years. Our day goes something like this: We get up early and have breakfast together. Then John tells me to go do my work, so I go upstairs to my office. I can't stand sitting at a desk for hours, so I do the laundry or something in the house. John does yard work and other things around the house, and he has an office on the lower level where he manages his investments. During the morning we talk on the intercom, meet for midmorning coffee and, of course, lunch as well. My workday is over at dinnertime. We can usually manage to stay awake to watch a 9:00 program on television, but 10:00 is just about the end of our day.

We have issues over some things. I wouldn't say we argue, but we do have pretty involved discussions because John's a Republican and I'm a Democrat. We have very different orientations, but we also respect the right of people to differ. We exchange a snide remark or a comment now and then, but we pretty much avoid encounters over political issues. We may be crisp in our comments, but I don't think either of us has ever actually raised his or her voice.

We work our money out jointly. I had a mortgage on my house, and John paid it off, so we now own it together. We have a joint checking account. I pay the bills, and John balances the checkbook. I don't like to balance a checkbook, and I'm not good at it either. Once I ordered some cologne, and when it came I said to John, "I didn't ask you if I could get this, did I?" He said, "You don't have to ask me. Of course, it's all right." We haven't had any issues about money. We're both very comfortable about the other person being fair.

I wouldn't say we argue, but we do have pretty involved discussions because John's a Republican and I'm a Democrat. We have very different orientations, but we also respect the right of people to differ.

JOHN: There was a period of about a year that my back gave me terrific pain. I was having trouble dancing, and that was depressing. Physical therapy took care of the pain for a while, but when it got worse my doctor took an MRI and told me there was no avoiding an operation. I had to do it. The surgery would also take care of a long-time problem in my left leg—a nerve problem coming from my spine. Now both problems are solved, and I'm in pretty good shape. I go to the gym at least twice a week and work out hard to stay in shape.

If one of us ever has to be responsible for the care of the other, we have an understanding of how to handle that. Pat and I both have spent a number of years as caregivers: me for my wife and Pat for her mother. And we both have long-term care policies and other coverage, which hopefully will ease the burden. We know that at some time in the future we're going to have to deal with this.

PAT: We've had several discussions about illness, end-of-life care, whether we want heroic measures. We have it all in writing. But we haven't had conversations with any of our kids about this, and we really need to do this sometime soon.

We've had several discussions about illness, end-of-life care, whether we want heroic measures.... But we haven't had conversations with any of our kids about this, and we really need to do this sometime soon.

Seven years ago John had prostate cancer. It left him with some physical limitations, and we've adjusted our sex life accordingly. Physical touch is important. We touch each other several times during the day, and we have our own private little jokes. For example, when we're walking up the stairs, whoever is the second one up the stairs gets to pat the fanny of the one in front. Little things like that are a source of pleasure and joy.

It may seem that I'm digressing, but I don't think I am. The best definition of loving I ever heard was when I was at a support group for couples many years ago. Some of the couples were grumbling about an unsatisfactory physical relationship, and an older gentleman got up and said loudly, "I need to tell you about love, because obviously you don't get it. After all the heat of passion dies down, it's what you have with each other that matters the most. The essence of love is the sharing and the caring. It's the respect, the love, and the honor. It's not the heat of the passion." That's how I look at our relationship. Physicality is part of any couple's intimacy. I wouldn't want to live together and not have touch as part of our being together. But it's not the essence of our marriage. We have a very precious relationship that isn't defined solely by sex. We know our lives aren't going to go on forever, so we go to bed at night and say the things that you want to say to the person you love the most. We listen to each other. I have some old issues, and John listens and gives me feedback and support. He has some old issues, and I listen and try to do the same for him. That's an important kind of intimacy we share.

Physicality is part of any couple's intimacy. I wouldn't want to live together and not have touch as part of our being together. But it's not the essence of our marriage. We have a very precious relationship that isn't defined solely by sex.

JOHN: We don't sleep together. I'm a blanket-stealer, and I had polio when I was young so I have restless muscles and move around a good deal. I'm a very restless sleeper. We each have visiting rights, though. I was afraid that not sleeping together might distance us from one another. I think that was a legitimate concern. My parents didn't sleep in the same bed, and many older couples we know sleep separately. It wasn't a lack of love but a necessity to get a decent night's sleep. It's not a threat to the relationship.

PAT: I am an advocate of people living together before they marry. It can make or break a relationship to experience the dailyness of life together. Everyone has old habits and personal idiosyncrasies, which is not necessarily good or bad, but you don't see how these affect living together until you try it. We lived together for three months before our wedding. During that time we faced a situation that gave me great confidence in our relationship. I had a mammogram with questionable results, and I said to John, "If this is bad news, I'm not going to hold you to marriage." And he said, "Hey, you don't ever have to worry about me, I'm in this for the long haul."

JOAN AND CHARLES

Charles is seventy-six. Joan is two years younger—she's seventy-four. These past four years they've had a long-distance relationship. Joan lives in the United States; Charles resides in Canada. This arrangement seems to work perfectly for them; in fact, they designed it that way. I didn't have to go to Canada to interview them, as this was a week when Charles was staying with Joan in her apartment. They had spent a couple of months together in Florida during the past winter, and before Charles planned to leave for his Canadian home in a few days I had a chance to talk with them.

JOAN: My husband died within six months of learning he had a terminal illness. It was a frantic time in which I tried very hard to continue to believe that he would survive. But I was the only one who had this desperate hope. I kept thinking that this couldn't be happening. Why is he getting worse and worse? I was in denial. He was a physician and knew very well the reality of his illness.

I was able to manage after his death, yet I felt terribly deprived after sharing my life with this man for forty years. My children and my friends were really marvelous in helping me, but I had to find a way to bear it and come out strong. One of the reasons I'm with Charles is that I've missed the connection of having a man in my life. I have friends who have lost their husbands and they remain unattached, but I couldn't live comfortably or happily that way.

CHARLES: My wife found she had cancer two years before she passed away. The first year was not so bad, she could function normally. We went on holidays, and she enjoyed them. But on our last trip she became very ill on the way home, and we went straight to the hospital when we got back. She told me she didn't want to die in a hospital, so I took her home and she passed away there. During that last period when she was home I had to do everything for her: bathe her, help with her personal needs. Luckily I could cook. My dear wife got the best of care and passed quietly away in my arms.

One of the reasons I'm with Charles is that I've missed the connection of having a man in my life. I have friends who have lost their husbands and they remain unattached, but I couldn't live comfortably or happily that way.

The initial grieving time was terrible. I cried my heart out. My wife and I had a long trip planned that, of course, we never took, and I decided to go by myself. It was the best thing I could have done. When I came back home, the worst part of my grieving was over, and I was able to resume my life. I wasn't looking for a companion. I didn't even think about that possibility. But it seems my friends did. One of them told me about a website called SeniorFriendFinder.com. I posted a profile of myself on line, and for a long time nothing happened. "Well, that's the way it is," I thought, and decided to forget about finding someone on the Internet. Then, one day, there was an e-mail from Joan. We started an e-mail correspondence and found we had a lot of things in common. Each of us had four adult children, had been married for forty years, and was widowed.

JOAN: I was very specific when I responded to Charles. I told him that I wanted a relationship with someone who didn't live in my community—but not too far away, either. Charles lived in Canada, five hundred miles away. Not too near, not too far. We corresponded for a while. Some of our e-mail letters were three or four pages long. We asked each other questions about religion and personal habits and many other things. Charles told me that he was a winemaker, and I shared with him that I make quilts. These are both solitary activities that take a lot of time, so he told me that we both must have patience. By the time we actually met, three years ago, we knew a lot about each other.

I wanted a relationship with someone who didn't live in my community—but not too far away, either.

CHARLES: We exchanged phone calls and e-mails for a couple of months, and then I decided to drive to where Joan lives and meet her in person. Both of us had been honest and forthcoming in what we told one another, so it wasn't like meeting a stranger. We had sent each other photos, but only face shots. I was looking forward to seeing what the rest of her looked like! We embraced and kissed when Joan opened the door. It was a good thing right from day one ... from the first minute!

JOAN: When I opened my door and saw Charles for the first time, I hugged him tight, and it has been great ever since. It was like hugging an old friend. How many people have the opportunity to know someone so well before they meet? It was marvelous all that weekend and has been for almost four years now.

CHARLES: We knew right from our first meeting that we would sleep together. We did have a moment of shyness the first time we undressed and got under the covers, but once we were in bed those apprehensions disappeared.

JOAN: Charles is a very different kind of person from my husband. Not that I'm making comparisons, but it's fascinating to have the opportunity to know another person intimately. I've had very few sexual partners in my life. I married in my early twenties. This relationship has given me an opportunity to experience another man's love.

Charles is a very different kind of person from my husband. Not that I'm making comparisons, but it's fascinating to have the opportunity to know another person intimately.

We discussed how we would set up our relationship and decided I'd visit him one month where he lives, and the next month he'd come here to stay with me. We originally arranged each month so we would have three weeks by ourselves and one week together. Now we see each other more because we've been going on long trips together. We've become very close. But we still like some time apart. For example, we took a three-week trip to Europe. Charles stayed here a week before we went and almost a week after we returned. We realized after five weeks together that we needed some time alone, and we've planned our relationship to allow for this. During our times apart we correspond on the Internet through instant messaging. And we can see each other. We have cameras on our computers. It's like having a face-to-face conversation. Although there are times when each of us wishes the other person was closer, each of us have "busy for old people" lives, with individual interests and friends.

CHARLES: Because we live apart, we each manage our own expenses. We're very fortunate that we're both independent financially. We each manage our own affairs, and we're comfortable. Seeking a new mate for financial security can lead to an unfortunate situation. We've established a common bank account, and on a monthly basis we each contribute an equal amount. That's our vacation money. So we save it and then we spend it!

JOAN: Knowing that I can be impetuous sometimes, one of my sons was apprehensive about my relationship with Charles. But now that he knows Charles, he knows that his mother has not made a foolish decision. If a person has had a good marriage, she should be open enough to try again. I've always been a thoughtful per-

People our age should not give up on their lives. I feel strongly that, regardless of your age, you need to reach out and have friends— maybe one particular friend ... like Charles.

son, and though I had a great desire to find an intimate companion, I don't think I ever sought a relationship out of a feeling of overpowering need or desperation.

People our age should not give up on their lives. I feel strongly that, regardless of your age, you need to reach out and have friends—maybe one particular friend ... like Charles. My view in the past was different. I thought that once you were widowed, your children became your only relationships. But that's a terrible burden to put on children. It's not that I don't enjoy their attention and love their concern for me, but I don't want that to be my life. And I don't want concern for me to be their lives.

I attribute some of the good relationship that Charles and I have to the fact that each of us has had long marriages. We've learned how to compromise without giving up our own self-esteem. We've learned to see the other person's point of view. I don't want Charles to be a male version of me. And I certainly don't want him to dictate what kind of a woman I should be. I would never give up my independence as an individual; I need to be who I am. But what we have together is so wonderful, so superb.

CHARLES: One of the biggest mistakes someone can make after their husband or wife dies is to remarry too quickly. Find a partner, but don't get married. Don't give in to social pressures or allow anyone to make you feel like you're living in sin. Every couple should make their own decisions about what they're comfortable with. In our case, we're both willing and able to understand the other, to share things together. Keep your common sense about the relationship—don't get so emotionally involved that you feel marriage is the only answer. Speaking from the point of view of the man, I don't need someone to run my house, do the cleaning and cooking. And we're certainly past the point of having babies. I'm not trying to change Joan, and she's not trying to change me.

I attribute some of the good relationship that Charles and I have to the fact that each of us has had long marriages. We've learned to compromise without giving up our own self-esteem.

JOAN: We have talked about the possibility of living together, but all of Charles's friends and family live in Canada. And although he enjoys the cultural activities here and the friends of mine that he's met, Charles doesn't want to live here full time. And I don't ever want to leave this city where I've always lived. Every time we've discussed living together we've come to the mutual conclusion that we enjoy it this way. When we're apart, we can do our separate things, and getting back together is always a new experience, and a new surprise. As Charles puts it, "Our coming back together rekindles the flame." This might seem a bit unreal, and on some level maybe it is, but it also is also very pleasurable.

CHARLES: But it does put off talking about end-of-life situations that will, of course, become part of our lives at some time in the future. We're not worried about future situations. We feel confident we will be able to work out what's necessary in whatever situation arises. I believe we're prepared to accept each other's problems in that respect. We're dealing with such a circumstance now. Joan had knee surgery recently, and while she was still in the hospital she had a stroke. I was here to care for her when she was released from the hospital. The stroke has affected her reading ability and to a lesser degree her speech. She confuses names that are capitalized, like cities and countries and names of people.

One of the biggest mistakes someone can make after their husband or wife dies is to remarry too quickly. Find a partner, but don't get married.

JOAN: I'm considerably better now than earlier this year. I'm hopeful there will continue to be improvement. I'm working seriously on strengthening the eye that is most affected. I can't read words that have more than four or five letters. Sometimes I guess at the word; sometimes I spell the letters I see out loud, and the word comes to me. Reading even a short newspaper article is time-consuming and frustrating, and I often lose patience. I have a special program on my computer that if I highlight a story, press a few keys, the computer will read it to me. It's been a comfort to have that to stay in touch with what's going on in the world. I also rely more on radio and television than I used to. Driving is an impossibility. I haven't sold my car, though. I just can't bring myself to do that, it would seem so final to me. It's all very frustrating to me. I'm a very healthy person otherwise.

We love our times together. We rarely disagree. Having arguments has no part in our relationship. That would deprive us of the pleasures. When we disagree about anything, it's something very minor. It's not at all important to our continuing relationship. We have a lot of fun together. We love to laugh. Before we go to sleep, we talk and giggle and laugh. I say, "I love you." I have a need to say it, and I need to hear his response, which is always, "I love you, too."

LILLIAN AND GEORGE

Lillian and George have been together four years, but they've known each other much longer. George has five sons and one daughter. George's daughter has Down syndrome and has always lived with her parents; she's almost fifty years old now. George is eighty-six. When I asked Lillian her age, she said, "A woman who will tell her age will tell everything." I told her that I had come hoping that she would tell me everything. "Oh alright, I'm ten years younger than George. I'm seventy-six," she confessed. George is Lillian's third husband. "I helped my first husband through medical school," Lillian told me. "George is a retired physician, so I understood what his work was and his commitment to it."

LILLIAN: I'm a woman of color. My grandfather on my daddy's side was half-Irish; my grandmother on my daddy's side was part French. On my mother's side, my grandmother was part French and part African. Her family was from the islands. She was dark-skinned. My grandfather on my mother's side was half-Indian. So I come with many mixtures of blood. I'm indeed a woman of color. When someone says, "What are we going to call you?" I say, "Call me Lillian. Or 'the woman of color.' Or if you can't get that straight, just say 'that lady over there in the red dress.'"

I've had an interesting and productive career. I've been around. I know who I am and where I've been. I've served this society, served my country, and served my family. I can't spend my time worrying about what people might think. When people see George and me together, mostly they glow. None of George's or my friends has given any indication that my being a woman of color and George being white is a problem for them. Maybe sometimes, when people are smiling at us, they're thinking, "That woman is a helper for that old man." The real situation is that we're together—head, soul, and body.

I know who I am and where I've been…. I can't spend my time worrying about what people might think.

I enjoy being a wife. I'd missed that. I feel good about being a companion and taking care of the household. If I have the strength and ability, I'll take care of George as long as I live. We've planned our days to give us the most comfortable life we can have at our age. George is older than I am, but I never want to see him in a nursing home. He has some trouble walking, especially on stairs, which is why we're living in a place with an elevator. And he can exercise right here in the building. There's a gym and a pool here.

GEORGE: I used to be a jogger, but I had to quit exercising for a while. I'm just getting back into daily exercise. I've had some swelling in my legs, high blood pressure, and a knee replacement. I also had cancer a while back, but I think I'm cured. I'm a little worried about my health, but I'm doing pretty good these days.

I first met Lillian almost forty years ago through a vocational training program that taught people ordinary living skills, like how to dress and other things, in addition to job training and placement. It was a well-designed social program that really accomplished something. When I called, a woman invited me to come by and see the place and learn more about the program. That woman was Lillian. She showed me around, introduced me to the staff—I was impressed. I joined the organization and began serving on the board of directors. Lillian eventually joined the board of directors, too. At that time I was married with a family of six children, and Lillian was divorced and raising her six children. She later remarried, but her second husband died after they were together twenty years. Lillian and I were friends and big supporters of a program that spent dollars wisely and put disadvantaged people to work. It's an ongoing program. I'm a retired physician,

I enjoy being a wife. I'd missed that.

but even when I was working I made time for volunteer activities for things I believed in.

LILLIAN: That's how I originally met George, many, many years ago. I had left a very good job to work for the program. It was an excellent equal-opportunity program that educated, trained, and placed workers and helped people get off welfare. A number of prominent people in the community supported it. George was physician, and some of his colleagues had told him about the program. When he called the office, he said, "I want to see if this is just another federal program wasting tax dollars." I invited him over to see what we had accomplished. We both ended up serving on the board for thirty-two years.

GEORGE: My wife passed away four years ago. I realized then that I really needed to be connected with someone. I have a daughter who has Down syndrome; she's forty-nine now. I was overwhelmed with taking care of both her and myself. I guess I was lonely, but I was too busy to give that much attention. Someone told me that my friend, Lillian, was moving to Arizona. That seemed awfully far for a friend of so many years to be moving. I told her we'd keep in touch and that we'd talk on the phone often and that maybe we could get together now and then. Lillian had written a column for many years for a locally published weekly newspaper, and she planned to write a book after she settled in Arizona. She wanted to be where it was warm and do the things that she'd had to put off for years while working to support her children through school.

My wife passed away four years ago. I realized then that I really needed to be connected with someone.

LILLIAN: As I was packing, George called and said he wanted to come over to talk. He sounded very serious. At one point he said, "I don't know if I'll ever marry again. I don't know how long I'll be in mourning. But I had planned to ask you to be my companion. We can take trips and do anything we'd enjoy together."

I had sold my house here and bought a new one in Arizona, and I was determined to move. I told George we'd stay closely in touch, but I promised him nothing. After I moved to Arizona, he called me every night. And I began to call him back. Our relationship grew deeper, and our conversations became more important to me. A short time later, one of my sons got married, and I came back here for the wedding. George asked me to keep my evenings free while I was here, and we spent a lot of time together during that visit. George came to my son's wedding with me. My children actually knew him from all the years we had been friends. So we wined and dined and had a lovely time together.

The last night before I was to leave to go back to Arizona, George talked at great length about how compatible we were, how much we enjoyed each other's company, and how he'd like to commit to a relationship. "What do you mean by 'commit?'" I asked. "I'd like to marry you," he said. "I want you for my companion and comrade."

So we were married. I can't say we were in love before we married, but we've grown into love. I do love George. He must have seen the caring in me, and probably some of the strength of his first wife. We're inseparable. In the winter we go to my house in Arizona, and in the summer we live here. George and I moved out of his large home, and we have this condominium now. Our relationship keeps growing deeper and better. George once said to me that there isn't anything we can't discuss and resolve, and he was right about that. We never want to hurt each other or make the other uncomfortable. We're totally honest with each other. We're good friends and best buddies. I think we're falling in love more and more each day.

I can't say we were in love before we married, but we've grown into love.... I think we're falling in love more and more each day.

I'm not a supersexual woman at my age, but I believe in myself and that inspires George to have confidence in himself. I believe I'm exciting for George. He thinks he's over the hill until I get close to him. Fires can be stirred! We cuddle and hug and kiss. We make love our way. People can show love in many ways. We can satisfy each other whether we're fully equipped to have traditional sex or not. Even at the age of eighty he can respond to whatever physical love I demonstrate to him. I know the limitations, too. Older people come together because they love each other, and sex isn't necessarily the top priority.

I'd never thought of George as a wealthy man. He was retired; I was retired. I figured we'd each have a pension and Social Security. Before we were married, though, George said we should make a prenuptial agreement. It was only then that I realized how well off he was. It was a surprise to me to find out that George owned more than the same old clothes he usually wore!

GEORGE: Lillian has resources of her own, but I pretty much support us. She actually has two houses in Arizona now; one is rental property. So her children will inherit what that is worth and what money she has. Lillian's children have been very accepting of me, and mine of her. We've set up a fair arrangement, I think. If I die before Lillian, she will be able to live comfortably, and my children will be beneficiaries as well.

I'm not a supersexual woman at my age, but I believe in myself and that inspires George to have confidence in himself.... Fires can be stirred!

LILLIAN: I'm drawn to respond to people in need. I could see that, because of her Down syndrome, George's daughter needed some help. I think I missed that part of my life—being needed. I saw how much this child needed a friend. She had no friends at all. When I met her, she was gaining weight because she just sat and watched television all day. When I would try to talk with her, she would respond with hand signals or shoulder movements. She didn't talk much at all. When I'd say to her, "Let's talk about what's on your mind," she'd reply, "Who cares?" I knew she needed someone to listen and pay attention to her, so I started to spend a good deal of time with her. I took her out to lunch once a week. I planned a birthday party for her. I taught her how to wash her clothes and do other things for herself. We became special friends.

GEORGE: What Lillian has done for my daughter is amazing. We thought we had taken my daughter as far a she could go, but Lillian really accomplished something wonderful with her. Sometimes my daughter says to me with great enthusiasm, "Where's my stepmother? I want to be with her."

LILLIAN: George's daughter lived with us for three years, but now she lives with one of her brothers in their family home. She's more comfortable being back in the house she knew for most of her life. And I realize now that I took on too much trying to care for her. I was stressed out, and my health was threatened. It was the first time I'd ever had to go on medication in my life. I realize now that I need to put my time and energy into my own health and taking care of George. I took on the challenge of caring for his daughter willingly. But, ultimately, it became too much for me. I feel good about what we accomplished together. She's happy with herself now. She still needs our love, of course, and I still take her out for lunch and a haircut and things like that. But it's better that she doesn't live with us anymore. George and I need all our energy for each other. We need to take care of ourselves at this time of our lives. It's like I said earlier. We're together in our heads, souls, and bodies. We're not just married, we're wedded. I love George, and I know he loves me.

We're together in our heads, souls, and bodies. We're not just married, we're wedded.

MERYL AND BOB

The romantic partnership of Meryl, seventy-eight, and Bob, seventy-nine, grows out of the roots of an old friendship. They've known each other since they were teenagers, though both were married twice in the intervening years. They have had an opportunity to reconnect in late life and are deeply committed to one another. But they can only be together when they make plans in advance. Meryl visits Bob in the United States from her home in Canada, and he often travels to Canada to spend time with her. Neither wants to leave their friends and family or the cities where they've lived for so long. "I guess we'll just continue this long-distance relationship," Meryl told me.

MERYL: We met sixty-four years ago, when I was thirteen. We got to know each other while waiting on the corner to take the streetcar to school. After school, Bob would walk me home, and then when he got to his house, he'd call me. Then we started going to the movies and dances and parties.

My mother worried that we were getting too serious about each other, that we were too young to be a couple. She warned me not to hold hands with him or kiss him or become emotionally involved with him. She told me that I shouldn't see Bob so much. I listened to her and did what she said, but the decision had repercussions. I went into a depression, though I didn't know the word for it at that time; I just knew I felt low and lonely. I didn't have another boy in my life until I was seventeen—a young man I knew came back from overseas. He had been in the Canadian Air Force in the Second World War and had been a prisoner of war. I was emotionally ready for any kind of loving. We started seeing each other, and we married when I was eighteen.

Here's a photograph I brought along to show you of my wedding. Bob was best man because he was a good friend of my husband, Norman. My best friend Pat was the bridesmaid. When Pat and Bob started going out together, Norman and I would often go with them. And then Pat and Bob married. That hurt me quite a bit. I guess I felt I never should have stopped seeing Bob. I also felt that if Bob had wanted to keep seeing me, we might have stayed together, even after my mother told me to stay away from him.

> *I guess I felt I never should have stopped seeing Bob [when I was a teenager]. I also felt that if Bob had wanted to keep seeing me, we might have stayed together, even after my mother told me to stay away from him.*

BOB: It wasn't that I didn't miss Meryl, but my life had changed. While my mother was visiting her sister in Boston, she broke her leg. She stayed with my aunt for three months to recover. I dropped out of school to take care of my sister, three younger brothers, and myself. I was the oldest child. My father was ill and an alcoholic, and we were very, very poor. I often thought about Meryl, but there wasn't much I could do to get back together with her.

When I was old enough, I joined the Canadian Navy. I was only in the service for ninety-two days before the war ended. After ninety days in the service in Canada, a person is eligible for educational benefits, so I started to catch up on the education I had missed out on. Meryl's friend, Pat, would come over and help me study, and I was able to quickly catch up. I got into the University of Illinois, then back to Toronto for my master's degree and later a Ph.D. in sociology. And that was the field I taught and worked in for my whole career.

MERYL: When Norman was incarcerated as a prisoner of war in Germany, he read a great deal and prepared himself for coming back and going to university. Only sixty out of two hundred applicants for Queens Medical School were accepted, and Norman was one of them. First, we lived in Kingston while Norman was in school, then Vancouver where he did his internship. By then I had two children. Later I had another child, but one of my sons died in his thirties, so only two of my children are still living.

I often thought about Meryl, but there wasn't much I could do to get back together with her.

BOB: While Meryl and Norman were living in Kingston, Pat and I got married. We moved from the University of Wisconsin to Cal State to the University of Minnesota as I got teaching jobs. Eventually I was appointed a full professor at the University of Minnesota, and this is where I've been for my entire career. Pat and I were divorced in the early 1960s, but we've remained friendly. In fact, the two of us are planning a birthday party for one of our three sons, who will be fifty years old soon. After my divorce from Pat, I remarried. Sadly, my second wife died of cancer when she was only thirty-seven, so I've been single now for twenty-seven years.

MERYL: After Norman and I suffered the loss of a son, we separated. When our divorce was final, I was sure I wouldn't seek another partner. But I did marry again. I met my second husband through Pat, who had returned to Toronto after she and Bob were divorced. My new husband had cared for his wife when she was ill and dying, and he had taken good care of his two teenage children through it all. I recognized that he was a good man. We built a life together. The kids grew up and went their own ways, and eventually he retired. We had many good years together, and then he developed Alzheimer's. He died seventeen years ago. My first husband, Norman, died fifteen years ago.

When Norman died, my daughter wanted me to be at the funeral. Bob and Norman had remained good friends, and Bob delivered the eulogy at Norman's funeral. I had thought about Bob many times over the years, and prior to Norman's death I had written to him. I still had deep feelings for Bob. It was a strange kind of connection I couldn't let go of.

I felt like I had been catapulted back to being a thirteen-year-old again. I knew I wanted to be with Bob. And Bob wanted to be with me.

Bob answered my letter saying that he'd be in touch as soon as he could get up to Toronto.

I felt like I had been catapulted back to being a thirteen-year-old again. I knew I wanted to be with Bob. And Bob wanted to be with me. The problem is, we live in different cities—actually, different countries. I'm in Canada, Bob's in the States. That's often painful for me. We take many trips together, and Bob comes back to Toronto from time to time, and I go often to stay with him.

BOB: We really have very different lives. As much as I enjoy being in Canada, I wouldn't want to live there. I've lived in the United States for almost sixty years, and my mother was American. I'm still a Canadian, but I have an American mentality. But we do see each other quite a bit considering that we live quite a distance apart and have so many obligations. When we're together several weeks and I take Meryl to the airport, I'm sad to see her go. It's an empty feeling when she leaves.

MERYL: It's the same for me. I feel cheated. I know there's no point in dwelling on it. I realized from the beginning that as much as I wanted to be with Bob all the time, my life is really in Canada. I've thought about moving to the States, but not seriously. Bob's life revolves around his work, his writing, and his friends. And my life is more centered on my children and my ten grandchildren. But I am conflicted because I want to be together with Bob more. That's the problem. It's been very frustrating at times, but I can't imagine either of us moving. It just wouldn't work.

I want to be with Bob more…. It's been very frustrating at times, but I can't imagine either of us moving. It just wouldn't work.

The first two years we were together were the hardest for me. I've come to terms with the reality of our situation now. We're increasing our time together, so the most we're apart at a time is maybe two months. And one other thing has changed: Bob and I talk on the phone every night. We share our day and our thoughts. This has made a great difference for me. But Bob's life seems complete without me. I don't really see myself fitting in anywhere except for visits. Bob has been working on writing a book for quite a long while, and the book is his mistress right now. Maybe when the book is finished Bob will need me more. Maybe then we can spend more time together.

BOB: I realize that I have less energy these past months for the research necessary to complete the book. I'm anxious to get it completed while I feel well and strong. I'm in relatively good health, except for a slow but active prostate cancer. And I have a bad leg, a restless leg that causes me to lose a lot of sleep. Sometimes I don't have the energy to get up in the morning to do the work. I'm afraid that I may not have the energy to finish the book, so I feel a great pressure to work as diligently as possible.

Meryl and I talk on the phone every evening. It's a new and comfortable routine that we've established. It's a good way to end the day. I always feel good when we've talked. And I always look forward to being with Meryl. She's a joy to be with—a wonderful woman. Meryl is a delight. She's calm, reasonable, and pretty—actually, beautiful. Getting together on this semi-regular basis is delightful for me. I welcome and anticipate our times together. And whenever Meryl is here, my friends want to spend time with her; they treat her very warmly. We laugh a lot. Meryl has a good sense of humor, and I'm always able to see the funny side of things. Humor is very much a part of our relationship.

I sometimes feel like my life has been one long getting ready so I could find Bob at the end of it.

MERYL: I sometimes feel like my life has been one long getting ready so I could find Bob at the end of it. Our physical relationship is a good one, and an active one. I wasn't expecting anything mild or tepid. People our age certainly have sexual relations, in spite of the myth that old people don't do that anymore. We hold hands in the movies, too, and hug even in front of our kids. I have as full an appreciation of Bob as if we had gotten together when I was seventeen! Our relationship completes me. I can't imagine being as happy without Bob in my life.

There are many little connecting links in our relationship that have accumulated over the years. In fact, our paths crossed so many times over the years that our families knew each other. At Norman's funeral my daughter commented to me that Bob's son said to her, "Wouldn't it be strange if our parents got together?" But even though our children and grandchildren seem comfortable with our relationship, we've decided not to get married—and not just because of the distance we live apart.

BOB: The decision has to do with proprietary issues. Our adult children don't necessarily welcome marriage, even if they welcome friendship, affection, and love. That's an issue for me. I've seen too many situations where the adult children have resented what they see as an intrusion in the family structure. They often resent another person having a legal contract with their parent, having a claim not only to the affections of the parent but to his or her property and money. I've seen negative reactions by children. I was the best man in a recent marriage of a friend, an older woman. The groom's daughter came up to a group of us later in the evening and said how difficult it was for her and the other adult children to accept the new wife after a marriage that had lasted for fifty-two years. I know you can't predict a reaction like this, but why invite it?

> *Our adult children don't necessarily welcome marriage, even if they welcome friendship, affection, and love.*

MERYL: I remember when I told my daughter that Bob and I were going on a trip together. She was happy for me, but she said, "You know, you don't have to make it legal, Mom." My son has the opposite feeling. He'd rather that I would make it "legal." I sense that he feels it would be the right thing to do. Bob and I have a very comfortable and loving relationship, but we're uncomfortable moving ahead in any legal direction.

BOB: Meryl and I try to make the most of each day. Our days together are delightful. We're very lucky that we have each other. We don't have the issues that younger people do: taking care of children, school, mortgage, financial stress, things like that.

MERYL: We have a lot of time just to be with each other, and in this respect, these are our golden years. We're not trying to plan a future. It's a privilege to have such happiness. We have today, and today is good.

LOUISE AND JAMES

James is seventy-two, and Louise is seventy-five. They have been living together for three years, choosing not to marry. How they met reflects the serendipity of many relationships. One day, a few years after her husband had died, Louise ran into a neighbor at the grocery store. "Come on, Louise, you have to get out," the neighbor said. "Come to the Labor Day singles picnic." Louise didn't seriously consider going, but when the day arrived she didn't have anything else to do, so at the last minute she decided to go to the picnic. It turned out to be a good decision for both her and James.

JAMES: I had heard that a singles group was having a Labor Day picnic. Before I went, I remember saying out loud to myself, "Aw, come on. Why do you want to go to the picnic all by yourself and admit your aloneness?" My wife had died two years before. Anyway, I finally went to the picnic telling myself I'd just stay a short while. I sat down at a picnic table, and Louise came along and sat down opposite me. We had a long, interesting conversation. I walked her back to her car but forgot to get her phone number. I remembered her last name, though, and looked her up in the phone book. She lived about three hundred yards from me, right across the street! I called her, and we made a plan to meet at a neighborhood coffee house. We were the last people there when they closed up. During that conversation I found out that Louise was a retired registered dietician and an avid bicycle rider. Let me tell you that I'm certifiably obese, and all I could think about was that a relationship would never work. But we started dating. I'd had a good marriage, and I guess I was looking for a relationship.

LOUISE: I wasn't really looking for a relationship. I was fine with being single again. It was James that pushed it. Over six months, more and more of his clothes started showing up in my closet, and I thought, "It seems like he's moving in with

James's lawyer told him not to get legally married, and my financial advisor told me the same thing. It gets too complicated with money and kids and all that stuff.

me." And that's exactly what happened. James has kept his condo and rents it out furnished. His daughter is in real estate so she handles that.

James and I have been together three years. We consider ourselves married now. We had a spiritual commitment ceremony. James approached a retired Episcopal priest and asked if he would perform the commitment ceremony. The priest asked, "Why do you want to do this?" And James told him, "We've got nine reasons—seven of mine and two of hers—and they're all grandchildren."

James's lawyer told him not to get legally married, and my financial advisor told me the same thing. It gets too complicated with money and kids and all that stuff. I have an adult son who is autistic, and I'll always need to provide for him. And if James should become ill, both my money and his could be depleted. So we decided not to officially marry, but we both feel a deep commitment about the relationship. Neither of us considers it a temporary thing.

JAMES: The priest said he was comfortable conducting the ceremony. He told us that in the eyes of the Church and God we were husband and wife. Now that we've made it formal, we feel we not only have an obligation to each other but to the community at large. In a way it actually places a bigger burden on our relationship because we've made a public commitment when we didn't have to. How do our children feel about our relationship? One of my daughters wasn't totally comfortable with it. She asked her sister, "Is Dad really happy?" And her sister replied, "Yes, he certainly is, so cool it!" Now she gets along well with Louise, and some of my grandchildren call Louise Grandma. One day we were sitting at a picnic table with the family, and my young grandson said, "Come on over here, Louise, I've got something for you." So she went around to the other side of the table and sat down next to him, and he leaned over and gave her a great big kiss. It takes a while for families to get to know a new mate, and we're lucky that our families have accepted the idea.

We decided not to officially marry, but we both feel a deep commitment about the relationship. Neither of us considers it a temporary thing.

LOUISE: I have two adopted children who are in their forties. I know now that my son is autistic, but when he was young they didn't really understand how to deal with autism, so he was sent to a school for the retarded until he was thirteen. He's now able to live alone, loves computers and mechanical stuff, but doesn't really have any friends or social life. He's a loner, but he really enjoys talking with James and calls him on the phone quite often, and that's fine with James. My son is unpredictable and erratic, and that can be an issue between James and me. But we don't really ever fight about things even though we have such different perspectives. I'm amazed that James tolerates my liberalism. Never once has he said that he wants me to believe as he does. That has really pleased and surprised me. We can have discussions without James trying to convince me that he's right and I'm wrong. We do get into some heavy discussions about politics. Maybe some people would call them arguments.

JAMES: I'm a Republican, and Louise is a Democrat. I'm not conservative to the point of being extremely right-wing, but I'm religious, and I know my scriptures. Our politics reflect our core beliefs and determine what causes we participate in. In this area, we've agreed to disagree.

I'm a Republican, and Louise is a Democrat.... In this area, we've agreed to disagree.

LOUISE: We basically just enjoy one another. We have lots of fun. I've always done a lot of physical exercise, and I really enjoy being active. We have a swimming pool right here in our complex, and at 8:00 in the evening it's almost always empty of other swimmers. That's when we go down there. Recently, James bought a bike. There's a large lake near us, and James rides around it once and I go around twice. He knows he needs to do this for his health. He's had a heart attack and now wears a pacemaker. He told me this morning he has a pain in his leg. It could be a circulation problem.

JAMES: Louise has brought me into the world of the hearing. My first wife was profoundly deaf. She didn't use sign language, but she did read lips. When we would go to see plays, she would read the script first so she had an understanding of what was going on. Louise and I go often to the theater and concerts and movies. I was involved in theater here in my community when Louise and I met. I told her, "Stick with me. I'll get you into show business!" We've done one show together, and that was great fun.

I encourage Louise to do things on her own as well. We don't always have to do things together. I think we're more interesting people when we go off on our own once in a while. Louise is taking Swedish lessons, and I'm taking an art class. That's something I never had done before. I've taken up sketching and drawing and working with pastels. Louise gives the appropriate ooohs and aaaahs when I bring something home that I've done in the class.

We both love to travel. On Louise's last birthday we were on a trip in Munich, Germany. Because it was a milestone birthday, I told the people at the hotel and they presented her with a cake inscribed "Happy 75th Anniversary." A birthday is really the anniversary of one's birth, so it made sense. And it was really nice to share the celebration with the forty folks who were on the Elderhostel trip with us. Recently, Louise took a trip with some of her friends to Peru. Three weeks without her here was a little too long for me. I really missed her. I won't put any constraints on her, but I hope from now on she'll take shorter trips when I'm not with her.

> *We don't always have to do things together. I think we're more interesting people when we go off on our own once in a while.*

LOUISE: James does most of the cooking, and he makes wonderful meals. Around 4:00 I'll say, "What's for dinner, dear?" He recently had stomach-stapling surgery and has lost thirty-five pounds. Now he eats much smaller amounts. We don't go out to dinner much, but when we do we order one meal.

James eats about a fourth of it because his capacity is so much less now, and I eat the rest. I've gained five pounds!

My first husband wasn't affectionate at all, and our sex life wasn't good. I didn't know much about sex until after we were divorced and I began dating again. Most of the men I was with during my single years were taking care of their own needs. My sexual relationship with my second husband was good, but with James it's very special. We really have good sex. He always puts my pleasure first. I love his tenderness, and we have a very loving physical relationship

JAMES: Before my wife's death, maybe fifteen or twenty years ago, I became impotent. I went through counseling and even had shots to help me get an erection. It was a frustrating experience, but my wife and I learned to live with it. She was very understanding. I told Louise about my situation, and she said, "Hey, that's no problem." And we proceeded to have wonderful sex. For me it was oral; for her it was manipulation. Sometimes it was oral sex for both of us. I can have an orgasm weekly, and Louise more like monthly.

My sexual relationship with my second husband was good, but with James it's very special. We really have good sex.

I discussed with my urologist getting a penile implant. The implant is made of plastic and has a little square pump that pumps fluid from a bladder into two tubes in the implant. It's very much like a natural erection, but it's mechanical. I wanted to be able to have "normal" sexual intercourse. I try to make sure that Louise is satisfied. I maintain that sex is important. It's a glue that holds things together, but it's not everything—it really isn't. I get a great thrill just holding Louise's hand or putting my arm around her and giving her a big hug, or walking into a group and saying, "This is my wife." I love Louise very much. Just this morning I said to her, "I think there's almost nothing better than going to bed with you except the pleasure of waking up with you."

We both realize that at some time in the future, there will be expenses connected with our health and eventually our deaths. I've put some CDs in a safety deposit box at my credit union for Louise. It was simple to set it up—a kind of insurance policy.

LOUISE: My last husband fortunately left me very comfortable. I am more financially secure than James. We know one of us is likely to die before the other, and I've been through it before. James, too, has had the experience of his wife dying and the expenses involved. A few years before I met James, I went to my lawyer and he encouraged me to put my condominium in my daughter's name. So I did, but now things have changed. If I die first, I want to be assured that James could stay here for at least a year. I need to make that arrangement. Or what if I need to go into a nursing home? As things stand now, I can't sell the condo; I don't own it. I guess I've got some things to think through because of my new life with James.

We freely talk about the relationships we had with our previous spouses. The one thing that we don't do is make comparisons.

JAMES: If you go into our bedroom, you will see on my nightstand a picture of my first wife and me. We were obviously very happy and had a good relationship. There are a number of pictures of my first wife here, and there are also pictures of Louise's second husband. We don't deny those relationships. It's fortunate that these relationships were good ones for both of us. There are no photos here of Louise's first husband. That marriage ended in divorce. We freely talk about the relationships we had with our previous spouses. The one thing that we don't do is make comparisons. We try hard to stay away from that.

MICHAEL AND ED

*When I met Ed, he told me that he'd had a long
committed relationship with a male partner in the past.
Michael, too, had been in a long relationship. Married for
more than twenty years, he is the father of two adopted
children. "It isn't like either of us was desperate to find a
new companion," Ed told me, "but I guess we were open to
it because we both knew how special it is to have a person
to share your life with."*

MICHAEL: I was living in Baltimore, a single person pushing
sixty, recently divorced. I had been married for twenty-three
years. I knew I was gay, but I loved children. Before I was
married, I tried to adopt and discovered that a single man,
certainly a single gay man, cannot adopt. Regrettably, my
wife and I had fertility problems, and she had two miscar-
riages. We ended up adopting two children. I guess it wasn't
fair to my wife that I never revealed my sexual preference, but
she did get two wonderful children out of the marriage.

My children are now twenty-one and eighteen. I think my wife had suspicions that I was gay, but she ignored them. She was angry with me after the divorce, but we get along better now. She realizes that my being gay wasn't a reflection on her in any way. I never was physically attracted to my wife, but I did love her. And I still love her.

Ed and I met online. It seems we were both fans of the television show *Survivor*. There was a message board about the show that each of us left a message on. After a while we began to exchange private e-mails with each other. Although I wasn't confident I could find a life partner this way, I did hope to meet someone I could trust, who shared the same values I have, with whom I could talk comfortably about many things, and who was also seeking permanent companionship. I was looking for someone I could love and who would love me and accept me for who I am. Some gay men are never going to be interested in a committed relationship, but others, like me, seek relationships with a permanent liaison in mind. Ed is a very attractive man. I've always been attracted to older men, and Ed is nine years my senior.

> *I never was physically attracted to my wife, but I did love her. And I still love her.*

ED: Michael lived in a different part of the country, so at first we didn't meet face to face. Yet we soon felt as if we really knew each other well through hundreds and hundreds of conversations that we had shared on our computers. We had many phone conversations as well. When we both admitted that we were getting serious about the relationship, we decided we'd better meet in person. We lived over a thousand miles apart, so I asked Michael to come and visit for a month.

MICHAEL: When I decided to come and meet Ed, I was really very worried that this wouldn't work. Yet, if we wanted to form a solid relationship, we had to meet and spend some time together to know how we both felt. If it didn't work, I would have learned a lesson about long-distance, computer-based relationships. But I didn't have any reason to fear, because when I drove up the driveway Ed was waiting and we embraced. We spent the first few weeks in non-stop talking. We needed to get to know each other completely and honestly, and we laughed a lot. It might seem like a strange way to meet and form a permanent relationship, but it worked out for us.

We had so many common interests and had gotten to know so much about each other before we actually met face to face that, when Michael arrived and we first saw one another, for me it felt like a celebration of reconnecting with an old friend.

ED: We had so many common interests and had gotten to know so much about each other before we actually met face to face that, when Michael arrived and we first saw one another, for me it felt like a celebration of reconnecting with an old friend. Yet I knew that if Michael moved to the city where I lived he'd have to give up easy access to his children, who lived in Baltimore.

MICHAEL: At first my wife thought it would be too much of a shock to my children for me not only to move across the country, but to live with a man. Of course, I had to tell them. I asked my kids to come to my apartment, and my wife came along because she was sure they would be traumatized and need her support. This was three years ago, and they were still both teenagers. I blurted our something like, "I'm gay and in love with a man, and I'm moving to where he lives to set up a life with him." There was a moment of silence, and my son said, "That's it? That's what you were so worried about telling us? We already knew."

My wife told the children that the Bible says that a homosexual union is forbidden. My daughter said she didn't think God would make something he hated. My son was more philosophical about it. He said that now he felt I was doing God's will, but when I was married to their mother I wasn't following the path God had for me. They seemed to be okay with it.

When my children came out here for Christmas last year and we picked them up at the airport, my daughter ran up to Ed and hugged him. I know many families have hard times dealing with similar situations because I belong to a group of gay fathers, and not everyone has a story of such comfortable acceptance. When Ed and I decided to move in together, we felt it was a marriage, so that's when my wife and I were legally divorced. We had been separated, but neither of us had filed for divorce. I keep in close touch with my kids. We e-mail a lot and talk on the phone about once a week. My daughter prefers phone calls. My son is in graduate school and lives with four other roommates, so he'd rather e-mail than try to have a phone conversation with all those people around.

I blurted out something like, "I'm gay and in love with a man, and I'm moving to where he lives to set up a life with him." There was a moment of silence, and my son said, "That's it? That's what you were so worried about telling us? We already knew."

ED: My father has passed away now, but before he died Michael and I used to go to the nursing home to visit him. My father started referring to Michael as my partner. We were very surprised, as he was a ninety-three-year-old man with a very conservative background. Someone once told me that parents always know, although he also told friends and relatives that I just wasn't "the marrying kind." I guess everyone really knew that I was gay, however, because at my father's funeral no one was surprised that I was with Michael. I was worried about my Aunt Golda for one, but to my surprise she reached over and held Michael's hand throughout the entire service. It brought tears to my eyes, because then I knew our relationship was accepted.

MICHAEL: When I went back to Baltimore for my kids' graduations—one from college, the other from high school—I stayed with my ex-wife, at her suggestion, in the house she received in the divorce. I wanted my kids to always have a place they could call home. That time in Baltimore gave my ex-wife and me some time to talk it all out. We needed to do that. I don't think she's bitter. She's happy with her life now, too. She has lots of friends, a good job, and she's social and active. My wife has come to accept my being with Ed. We've gotten past the anger stage.

At my father's funeral, Aunt Golda ... held Michael's hand throughout the entire service. It brought tears to my eyes, because then I knew our relationship was accepted.

Most people seem to accept us. Every once in a while someone at the supermarket will give us a critical look when we're shopping together, but we ignore it. I remember one time when I took the train back home from visiting my kids in Baltimore. When I got off the train, Ed was there to meet me, and we embraced and kissed. Some woman gave us a critical look. It wasn't that important to us; we just ignored her. We figured that it's her problem, not ours. I guess in some situations there might be a little bit of shock displayed, but for the most part I think people just ignore us.

I'm a retired teacher by profession. I taught first through third grade over the years. What I do now is work at a gay library. It's the third largest such library in the country. Almost all of the material in the library deals with gay and lesbian issues and related areas of interest. My church serves an inner-city population and provides tutoring for children who are having learning problems at school. My other job is working there as one of the tutors.

Retirement is really nice, but you just can't sit around all the time. We do many things together. We enjoy going shopping, going to concerts and plays. And church activities keep us quite busy. I've just registered for a weaving class. That's something I've always wanted to do. And Ed is a painter. Although he has neglected that interest for a while, he's going to get back to it now. We both have leisure time, and we want to fill it with creative activities that we enjoy.

ED: We don't have money problems. The part-time jobs that Michael has don't bring in much income, but we pool our money and get along. I'm getting Social Security but am still employed part time as a graphic designer, which is the kind of work I've done for many years. We pool all of our money, and Michael takes responsibility for paying the bills. We don't worry

Retirement is really nice, but you just can't sit around all the time.... We both have leisure time, and we want to fill it with creative activities that we enjoy.

about who spends what. Sometimes if it's a big expenditure we discuss it first. We've replaced all the furniture in our apartment with things we've purchased together so it's our stuff in our home. We don't live extravagantly, so the money works out fine.

MICHAEL: The only area of disagreement we have is Ed's need to collect stuff. Our spare bedroom is full of things he can't seem to get rid of. I'm a minimalist; our styles are very different in this regard. I don't save a lot of stuff. I'm uncomfortable having that much clutter around. But we've worked out a compromise: Ed has agreed to keep his stuff all in one room so the rest of the place looks neat. That's how we solved the problem. That extra room is all Ed's. I don't even go in there. That's how we solved our biggest problem.

ED: As far as our styles of keeping house ... well, I confess, it irritates me that Michael uses the floor as a bookshelf. The floor seems to fill up with books and papers. But stuff like piles of books are small things in our relationship. Anything else that comes up that's an area of disagreement, we just talk it out. We're good about that.

MICHAEL: We have nicknames for each other. Ed is "Boo," and I'm "Puppy." I don't know how these nicknames even came about, but when we're alone we use them a lot. Sometimes we just refer to each other as "dear," "sweetie," or "hon." "Hon" is a common Southern term, and I was brought up around people from the South. I do a lot of the cooking, and it's Southern-fried everything. I like to cook okra, fried green tomatoes, and greens, but these greens make Ed turn green!

We have shared values. The church is very important to us; our religion is a big part of both of our lives.

ED: Michael does most of the cooking. We break up the household chores, and I do the heavy stuff because of his sensitive back. We automatically took on what we each do best.

There are great rewards in this relationship for me. I'm very happy with what we have together. We have shared values. The church is very important to us; our religion is a big part of both our lives. I now have someone to share intimate, honest conversation with, to hug and feel close to—a best friend to plan vacations with, to share a home with, and to love.

Michael took early retirement and went on disability after he'd had six back operations for a damaged spine. His last surgery was just three months ago. So he has Social Security and a pension from his teaching career. He also has prostate cancer. Michael takes daily medication and has to get a shot every four months. So far he seems to be in what I think they call a chemical remission.

MICHAEL: Ed doesn't have any major health problems, but we've planned ahead by having advance directives and legalizing a health care power of attorney. You have to do that if you're a gay couple so you can make decisions about the care of the other. If I can't make my own decisions, there will be no question that Ed is the person who will make them. My children are aware of that.

Gay men always worry that they're going to end up growing old alone, but now Michael and I have each other. I don't want you to think Michael and I got together because we don't want to be alone. We put our lives together because we loved each other and wanted to be a couple.

ED: I'm sure one of us will end up taking care of the other eventually. I actually look forward to that. Gay men always worry that they're going to end up growing old alone, but now Michael and I have each other. I don't want you to think Michael and I got together because we don't want to be alone. We put our lives together because we loved each other and wanted to be a couple.

We belong to a Lutheran church that's very gay friendly. In fact, it was people who weren't gay who pushed for the church to become a reconciling church and also to form a gay and lesbian alliance within the church. Although I was Methodist, I quickly joined Ed's Lutheran church because it was so comfortable for me. Our congregation is considering blessing same-gender unions. We plan on being one of the first couples to receive such a blessing in our church. It would legitimatize our relationship in the eyes of the congregation. I want my children present for that and also our friends so they can share our joy of being together.

MICHAEL: And when I say my goodnight prayers, I'm always grateful for our coming together. God must have known we needed each other.

SANDY AND HERB

*I met Sandy a couple of years ago. She was the director of the Department on Aging in her city; that's how we became friends. She retired seven months ago at the age of sixty. "I've worked since I was twelve," she told me, "so I decided to take early retirement and explore a different way of living. That change didn't necessarily involve looking for a mate," she told me with smile, "but now I share my time with Herb. I guess you never know what might come into your life. Herb and I knew each other many years ago."
Herb, sixty-two, wasn't seeking a woman to share his life. "I wasn't really looking for a companion," he told me, "but when Sandy and I reconnected, it just seemed right."*

SANDY: For many years, my work was my life. I'm retired now, and I miss the friendships I had but not the work itself. I'm very grateful that I was able to retire when I did. Two very close friends of mine died at the age of sixty-one. Before one of these friends died, she asked me to move in with her.

She wasn't at all well, couldn't work anymore, and was frightened she might lose her house. I went to live with her as her caregiver until the end of her life.

The deaths of my friends convinced me to have a different life, so I decided that sixty was going to be my last year working. I'm open now to new and different experiences. I'm going forward and doing the things I want to do.

Herb and I met for the first time when he was sixteen and I was fourteen. We used to go for long walks, hold hands and talk, and talk, and talk. We did that off and on for a couple of years, and then he went off to college and the military, and we hardly saw each after that.

About a year ago, Herb's cousin, who has always been a very close friend of mine, called and told me that Herb's dad had died. I went to the visitation at the mortuary, and as I was leaving, Herb was on the steps waiting for me. He opened up his arms, and we shared a big hug. He told me that seeing me again was a bright spot in his life. He told me that during the past year he had lost both of his parents and five other close relatives and a good friend.

> *Herb and I met for the first time when he was sixteen and I was fourteen.... Then he went off to college and the military, and we hardly saw each other after that.*

HERB: I've had seven deaths in my family in the last year— both of my parents, an aunt, uncles, cousins—and my best friend died as well. There aren't many people I can open up to and talk about the loss of my mother. My mother and I were very close. For a while I was numb; now I'm starting to hurt. I feel like an orphan with so many of my family gone.

SANDY: The week after seeing Herb again I called him to see how he was doing, and to my surprise our conversation lasted over four hours. I didn't think I wanted a relationship with a man, but seeing Herb and talking so comfortably with him got me thinking differently. I thought, "Maybe there's something here." I had never forgotten him. The previous year, as I was cleaning, I had come across some old photographs. Most of the pictures of my high school pals I had tossed out thirty or more years earlier, but Herb's graduation photograph was still there in my drawer. I had saved his photo. One day very recently Herb showed me an old picture of myself that he had saved. I had given it to him when he was home on leave from the Air Force in 1965.

We'd both been alone a long time. I'd been divorced for almost eighteen years; he'd been divorced thirteen years. I have three children: twin daughters who are thirty-four and a son who just turned thirty-nine. I wasn't looking for a mate, just companionship, someone to go fishing with (which my women friends weren't interested in doing). And sometimes I just wanted to go somewhere with a man. I probably wouldn't have been open to another relationship, but Herb and I already knew each other, and we easily reconnected. My children were very excited when I told them about Herb. They all expressed the feeling that it was about time. Herb and I have been together a year now.

Sandy and I live in separate houses in different cities, yet we manage to spend quite a bit of time together.

HERB: I'm so comfortable with Sandy. I can tell her everything, talk about my feelings, and that's been so good. Sandy helps me a lot, gives me support—and gives it freely. She's a good listener. Sandy and I live in separate houses in different cities, yet we manage to spend quite a bit of time together. I like the town she's living in better than where I live, so I visit her more often than she visits me. I've known Sandy's ex-husband for many years. He actually lives across the street from me. It's an unusual situation. We've never really been on comfortable speaking terms. We're kind of oil and water. I think he's still jealous.

SANDY: Herb comes and stays with me once or twice during the week. I often go to his place on the weekends. We're both used to having alone time, and we each need that. But sometimes, when we're not together, we get lonesome, and then we end up spending a lot of time on the phone. The most important thing Herb and I have together is our friendship. It's a genuine liking, and there's total trust. We've told each other everything about our lives. We're really best friends. We're always considerate of one another, and we like to do things together. That's a great basis for a relationship. We've never discussed marriage, yet we both have demonstrated a real commitment to one another.

We've never discussed marriage, yet we both have demonstrated a real commitment to one another.

HERB: I've been unable to work for a few years because of family difficulties. My aging parents lived in another part of the country, and I needed to be there to assist them. That started about ten years ago. The caregiving wasn't full time at first, but then I started getting phone calls telling me to get back quick, take a plane as fast as I could. This happened so many times that I just stayed with my parents. It didn't work to be a full-time caregiver and try to hold down a job, too. Now I'm looking forward to getting back into the work world. Meanwhile, I do subsistence work. I paint houses, fix windshield chips, stuff like that. I'm not sure whether I consider myself retired or not.

SANDY: Herb just started drawing his Social Security, and he supplements his income with the temporary jobs he's been finding. I'm getting my retirement benefits now as well. As for managing our finances … when he can contribute, he does, and when he can't, I do. It works out naturally and comfortably. Money hasn't been an issue between us at all. Herb may think I'm contributing more because I've been taking him out to restaurants for fancy dinners, but I'm using the many gift certificates that I was given when I retired.

HERB: We haven't formally worked out the money thing, but she contributes more than I do. It isn't a stumbling block in our relationship, but I hope I can be more of a stand-up guy about money in the future. We've been going a lot to restaurants, but I really like to cook at home. I've learned to cook from friends who are professional chefs, and I'm a really good cook. Sandy loves to go fishing. She catches the fish, and I cook them.

I try to make the most of every day. I concentrate on enjoying the moment.… I don't make long-range plans. One day at a time, that's it.

I don't have any children. I think Sandy's children like me. I like them, and they've accepted me. She's got grandchildren, and it's nice to be with them. I try to be thoughtful and attend family functions, and they seem to appreciate that.

SANDY: Herb has a wonderful sense of humor. We laugh a lot. It seems like we laugh eighty percent of the time we're together. We always have a good time, even when we're doing nothing. I try to make the most of every day. I concentrate on enjoying the moment. I've learned to do this from working with older people for so many years. I don't make long-range plans. One day at a time, that's it.

When we first started seeing each other, Herb hadn't been taking care of himself at all. He'd been a caregiver for so long, all he thought about was doing what needed to be done for his parents. I knew he had been a wonderful caregiver for them, but he paid the price of not taking care of himself. In my work with aging I've seen this happen too often.

HERB: I got very sick with viral flu the day after Sandy retired. That was six months ago, and I'm just beginning to feel better. My voice still hasn't come back all the way. Sandy took real good care of me. We've taken care of each other during illnesses. When she had a cornea transplant this spring, I moved in and took over until she could get along on her own again. Now we've started to go with each other to medical appointments.

We started out more physical than we are now; it was more sex to begin with. Now we're getting into more hugging and holding.... I've been very self-conscious about my body, but recently I'm feeling better and looking better, and I'm gaining self-confidence.

SANDY: I had two hip replacements seven years ago and gained twenty pounds, so I don't feel very good about my body these days. I used to go to the gym and run every day. I can't do that anymore because I have a pin in my right hip. But I stretch and do tai chi, and I hope to do more exercise soon. I gave up smoking recently, and that's another healthy thing. I'd like to start playing golf again, and go fishing, of course. One day at a time, that's how I figure.

I know my body doesn't look like it did forty-five years ago when Herb was first attracted to me. That has been difficult for me. It's been difficult for me, not having a physical relationship for such a long time. We're still easing into the physical relationship to a certain extent. We're both still a little standoffish and private. We started out more physical than we are now; it was more sex to begin with. Now we're getting into more hugging and holding. Touching is very nice. I like to be touched. I've been very self-conscious about my body, but recently I'm feeling better and looking better, and I'm gaining self-confidence. We have patience with each other. Herb is very giving, caring, and sensitive.

HERB: Sandy has been so thoughtful and good to me over this past year. I try to be as helpful as I can be. She has a cabin in the middle of a forest by a river. I do stuff there that needs fixing. I grew up doing that kind of stuff so I'm very good at all of that.

As far as our relationship goes, I always remember to give enough so I don't feel selfish. When I'm not at Sandy's house, I call her every morning at 8:00. And the first one who goes to bed calls the other one to say goodnight.

BARBARA AND STEVE

Neither Barbara nor Steve was looking for a new relationship when they met. Barbara told me that she still had a lot of healing to do: "The pain of my divorce had left me raw." But relationships have a surprising way of growing on their own. Steve agreed to be interviewed for this book when Barbara indicated she was eager to share her story. He had just turned sixty-five; Barbara is five years younger.

STEVE: I'd been divorced for many years and was living with another woman, who was considerably younger than me, nineteen years younger to be exact. It wasn't working for either of us, or for our families. I left the relationship and got a new job. My life became going to work, coming home, eating, and watching television. I was living temporarily with a friend of my son because he lived close to my parents' home and they were both ill. I was taking care of them. It seemed like I needed more in my life. I was lonely and decided to reach out and find a way to connect with other people my age.

I mentioned to a colleague at work that I was ready to have a relationship. I just meant somebody to talk to, somebody to have dinner or go to a movie with—a friend who was comfortable and reliable. I didn't mean that I wanted a serious relationship. But I kept running into this guy at the office, and he kept saying, "Oh, you have to meet this great woman. You two are both physically active and have a lot of the same interests. She's just gone through a divorce and is having a hard time." So he called Barbara and told her about me, a guy from work who wanted a relationship. "I'm NOT interested in a relationship!" she told him emphatically. "I'll just go to dinner with him, thank you." I guess the word "relationship" means something different to a woman. All I wanted was to go to dinner as well.

We made a plan to meet at a restaurant, got seated at a nice table on the patio, and the first thing Barbara said to me was, "I don't want a relationship. I'm not interested in a relationship." So the boundaries were set. During the next four hours I discussed my divorce and recently terminated relationship, and I told her lot about myself. It was an enormous relief to talk and to have someone actually listen. I went home and slept for sixteen hours, I was so exhausted. I had been living basically in silence and under a lot of stress. Barbara gave me the opportunity to unload a great weight. We were both self-disclosing, and we quickly discovered our common bond of pain. We ended up calling ourselves a couple of wounded birds seeking to learn to fly again.

I had been living basically in silence and under a lot of stress. Barbara gave me the opportunity to unload a great weight. We were both self-disclosing, and we quickly discovered our common bond of pain. We ended up calling ourselves a couple of wounded birds seeking to learn to fly again.

BARBARA: Nothing had ever happened in my life that was as painful as my husband leaving me. We had been married twenty years. The hurt I experienced was deep and profound. All the little betrayals and desertions throughout my life were magnified. I resisted even the thought of entering into a new relationship. I was concentrating on me, on healing and trying to put the pieces back together in my life. I don't know quite how Steve and I got together. He just started turning up where I was. When I went to my yoga class, there he was. We had only one official date. The rest of the times he'd just show up, and we'd go to dinner and spend time together. I felt very neutral about him. After all he was short and bald and older than I was. I kept telling my friends that if I ever ended up in a relationship the man had to be at least five years younger than me and tall. He certainly wouldn't look

Nothing had ever happened in my life that was as painful as my husband leaving me.

like Steve. But I was very impressed with Steve's caring for his parents and his devotion to his children. It was wonderful to see how important his family relationships were to him—very different from my husband, who took care of his aging parents out of duty. Steve did it out of love.

STEVE: I've always had a space issue, a touch issue. My mother felt love for me, I'm sure, but I learned from her not to be a physically demonstrative person. I've always had that problem. Here's the story of how things changed for me. I was on my way to pick Barbara up. I was driving down a little side road, and I saw a motorcycle on its side and a young man lying in the grass. I had been a medic in the Air Force so I was reasonably comfortable in such emergencies. I could see that both of his legs were broken and he was in great pain. I got down on the ground, stayed very close to him, and assured him that help was on the way. I stayed there until the ambulance came and took him away. During that whole time I was totally composed and comfortable, but after the ambulance drove away, the gravity of the situation started to sink in, and when I got to Barbara's house I had kind of deer-in-the-headlights look. I said to Barbara, "All I need you to do is hug me." I was willing to let go of being totally self-reliant, and I reached out and asked for help and comfort.

It was a pivotal moment in my life and in our relationship. We had probably not touched at all during the months we spent time together. That was pretty much the turning point for us. Now we've been together for three years, and we're committed to being life partners. We live together and do almost everything together except our work. We go to family gatherings together—spend time with Barbara's siblings and cousins and join my family at their events as well. We've even blended in some ways with my former wife. We're aware we come from different worlds. Barbara is Catholic; I'm Jewish. She's from a family of twelve. I

> *I said to Barbara, "All I need you to do is hug me." … It was a pivotal moment in my life and in our relationship. We had probably not touched at all during the months we spent time together.*

have a family of two. I have two married children and four grandchildren. Barb has one son and two granddaughters. My family is very, very private. Barbara's is very open and disclosing. Often she'll ask me questions like, "How do you feel about that?" I tell her I don't know how I feel. I just don't have words for feelings. I never learned that in my family. That has been an issue for us, and it remains an issue.

I think one of the things that brought us together in terms of a common bond is that I started going to church with Barbara. It wasn't so much about searching for God or looking for some kind of a religious connection, it was about spending that hour with Barbara in a place where I had quiet and solitude and the opportunity for reflection. It was a place that offered me a strong feeling of connection with Barbara. We were together in the same space, and it became a meaningful part of our lives. Mass has been a place for growth and meaning in our lives together.

BARBARA: We talk about marriage, but I'm Catholic and there are all kinds of repercussions in the church to getting married again. I think, too, that it would be really hard for my dad if I married Steve. Part of me would like the world to know that we're committed—to say, "He's my husband"—although it already feels like that. We feel like we're married.

Part of me would like the world to know that we're committed—to say, "He's my husband"—although it already feels like that. We feel like we're married.

STEVE: I'm in a complex situation. I abandoned my wife. I left her for another woman, and I will carry the guilt and the hurt of that for the rest of my life. And then I meet Barbara, and she's carrying that pain of having someone leave her. So I feel it twice. I feel the pain for her and for the wife I left. When Barbara found out that her ex-husband had remarried, she suffered weeks of pain. It was like having open-heart surgery a second time. I don't want to hurt Barbara by not marrying her, but neither do I want to hurt my ex-wife by marrying Barbara. It's a struggle for me. Yet I feel like we're married. I don't know whether to have a wedding with three hundred people, run off to Las Vegas and get married, or just continue on as we're living now.

BARBARA: I never have an uncertainty in Steve's feelings for me. There's a steadiness in our relationship, which is what I want, what I need at this time in my life. For the most part, there's a serenity and comfort in our relationship, and a stability that we both want and need. We had sex about three or four months into our relationship. The physical part of our relationship has some importance for me, but it doesn't necessarily have to be the sex act. In our twenties we were controlled by our hormones. Now, other things matter.

We went for a walk this morning for almost an hour, and we held hands all the way. If I had to choose between that walk just holding hands and having some Fourth of July sex experience, I'd take the walk. It's not to say that sex isn't important; I love having sex. But I think it's important not to equate intimacy with sexuality. Our first year together was very bumpy. Having sex is a part of our relationship, but it's not the most important. More important are the small things, like sitting out on our deck with a glass of wine and a good meal and comfortable talk. That's intimacy.

The physical part of our relationship has some importance for me, but it doesn't necessarily have to be the sex act. In our twenties, we were controlled by our hormones. Now, other things matter.

STEVE: I don't know whether sex is a road to intimacy or intimacy is a road to sex. I guess a full relationship is both. We've had some difficult times sexually. Some of this is psychological and some physical. Things just don't work they way they used to for me. It's like having an old car. I want to step on the gas and go faster, and it just doesn't do it. I have the drive and the want, but I also have the fear that when I step on the accelerator, it's probably going to go nowhere.

I love Barb when I see her out in the garden picking flowers. I love her when I see her sleeping next to me. I love her when she says; "I'm ready to go, I'll be there right away," and then I stand waiting by the door for ten minutes. I can't seem to say the words "I love you" in the way Barb would want to hear them, but I do love her deeply. I do.

BARBARA: I have no doubt of Steve's love, no doubt at all, even if the words "I love you" catch in his throat. There's a sense of calmness in our relationship. I don't need fabulous trips or all sorts of stimulation. The way we live is to me what life is about. There's something about our relationship, not wanting it to be something else, not worrying about if it will end, and knowing we have a commitment for as long as we're alive. I'm truly grateful for what I have today. I never would have dreamed of having this life five years ago when my husband left and I felt like my world would be empty forever.

STEVE: There's one area of our relationship that is troublesome for me, the financial situation. In reality, money is an issue. Barbara is very secure. She owns this house we live in. At this point we divide expenses equally. I contribute to the upkeep of the house, both money and sweat equity. I don't want to be looked at as someone who is taking advantage, and I sure don't want to be a burden on anyone. I should have planned better in my younger years and thought about my financial needs in retirement, but I didn't. I'm working so I have an income and do contribute, but the financial thing still is an issue.

I'm truly grateful for what I have today. I never would have dreamed of having this life five years ago when my husband left and I felt like my world would be empty forever.

BARBARA: Steve has a good job, but he works hard and puts in long hours. It's the kind of job you would take on when you're forty and on the way up, not when you're sixty-five. It's interesting and challenging for him, but it's stressful and demanding. When we were first involved, I was angry that he didn't take care of his financial situation earlier in his life. I know now that he isn't as bad off financially as he implied, and I think if there's no catastrophe to deal with he'll be able to manage. We've often talked about money, sure, but lately it hasn't been an issue. The biggest problem that we've had and probably will continue to have is the financial disparity. For me it doesn't really matter. I don't mind picking up the tab for some things, that's fine. The challenge in the future is going to be to do things I want to do. I want to travel, and that costs money and I know Steve doesn't want me paying his way. I could easily pick up the tab for our travel, but it makes me kind of mad that Steve didn't take care of financial security for his future. There's this part of me that says, "You're going to reap what you didn't sow!" I guess I could end up traveling with my sisters, but that isn't what I really want to do. But I'm sure not going to let this relationship fall apart over money. That would be ridiculous. This man gives me more than money can ever give me. I'd rather be lying in bed next to him than a pile of money.

I'm sure not going to let this relationship fall apart over money.... This man gives me more than money can ever give me. I'd rather be lying in bed next to him than a pile of money.

My divorce taught me more than any other experience in my whole life—about myself, about people, about the world, about everything. I'm very different today than I once was. The feeling of calmness in my relationship with Steve is a delight for me. What we have together is what life is about. I don't worry like I used to that feeling good or happy had a flip side of loss. I waited for it all to fall apart. It's about appreciating what we have today. Just the other day Steve gave me a refrigerator magnet that says, "Love as if you've never been hurt before." I think it was the universe speaking to us to help us heal our hurt.

STEVE: Now I try to live fully each day. We go out for a walk in the morning, and I can smell the petunias and there's dew on the grass. Just to take in the beauty of the world is wonderful. But you can't have an experience like that every day because life isn't that way. Maybe there's sand in your shoe or something unexpected that comes up, or having to get to work, or thinking about family concerns, or whatever. Fortunately, we don't have any young kids that we're worrying about. And although we both have jobs, we're not putting energy into building our careers. Neither of us is trying to climb the corporate ladder. We've had careers. At this time of our lives we're in a place where we can be more of what and who we are individually, and put our energy into growing as a couple. It's about being; just being yourself—and be comfortable with who you are. You come to understand and appreciate both your strengths and your weaknesses as you get older. I accept that I'm not who I was; I'm discovering who I am now. I can say to myself that I can appreciate who I am, and I don't have to beat myself up for what I'm not. And you can do the same thing with a relationship. You can "be" in that place with another individual, and you can know that the relationship feels good. It's not what it isn't, but what it is. It's difficult to explain feelings, but I'll try. Maybe it's a feeling of a calm sea or a field of grain without wind.

You come to understand and appreciate both your strengths and your weaknesses as you get older. I accept that I'm not who I was; I'm discovering who I am now.

BARBARA: I have the awareness that life has a way of changing everything you thought or planned. When I was younger I never saw things that way. I guess I felt that I was more in control of everything. Maybe it's maturity but now, as far as taking each day as it comes, there's more of that in me than ever before. I think I've changed and grown because of my age, the heartbreak of my divorce, and my love for Steve. I've learned more about myself, about other people, about everything. I'm very different today in my awareness than I used to be. I feel like the luckiest woman on this earth.

STEVE: Both Barbara and I have a new sense of comfort with ourselves. I guess maybe I'm describing something that, if you're lucky, comes with age. I'll simply say that I'm humble and grateful for what I have today, for what we have today. We've both grown both separately and together. We started out with neither one of us wanting a relationship, and here we are together in a partnership that has stability and serenity and, we believe, permanence.

GRACE AND AMELIA

When I began my conversation with Grace and Amelia, I asked if their friends and others accepted an intimate relationship between two older women. "Our relationship has always been honorable and dignified. We love our life together," Amelia told me, "and others get the sense that we have a good life." Amelia is sixty-five, and Grace is seventy. On her birthday, Amelia gave Grace a diamond ring. "The ring is deeply meaningful to me. I'm a big believer in ritual and tradition," Grace told me with a tear in her eye and smile on her face. "We're both very proud of each other and of our relationship. Maybe being older has made us less concerned how the world views our being together."

GRACE: I had been married to George for twenty years when I met Amelia. George and I weren't living together at the time, but we were still good friends, and I often spent time in the summer at his place. We both were artists, and we had a studio there. It was a more isolated, rustic place than where

I lived in the city and a lovely place to concentrate on our work.

How did I meet Amelia? It was at a reception at a local art gallery where some of my art was on display. Amelia was one of many people attending the art show. I was circulating around the room, and I walked over and chatted with her. My husband, George, joined our conversation and invited Amelia to a fish fry that we were having that evening after the gallery closed. Our relationship developed the way most good friendships do. We shared a lot of interests, and we started spending time together. No matter where we went we had a lot of fun and enjoyed each other's company. But in addition, I felt a physical attraction for Amelia that I had never experienced before.

I certainly wasn't looking for a new relationship. I've always had a very full and rich life. I have my art and my teaching and my children. George and I have a grown son in his forties, and I have another son from my first marriage, who is almost fifty now. Yet, though there was an attraction in both my marriages, a deep intimacy was always missing from my life. I sometimes think of the anthropologist Margaret Mead, who had three committed relationships. Her first was for children, her second was for intellectual exchange, and her third was for love. That third relationship was with a woman. Once I was attracted to Amelia, I never felt a physical attraction for another man or woman. Sometimes I think that this is what mating for life is supposed to be. If something should happen to Amelia, I would always know that she is for me what some call a "soul mate."

> *Our relationship developed the way most good friendships do. We shared a lot of interests, and we started spending time together.... In addition, I felt a physical attraction for Amelia that I had never experienced before.*

AMELIA: I had been divorced for about six years and recently ended a relationship, and I wasn't looking for someone to love or to love me. I had everything I needed in my life. I had two children, many friends, a great job as a film producer, and a community of colleagues. I guess I was feeling rather smug that my life was complete without a romantic attachment.

When Grace and I became friends, we started going places together. One night we attended a concert where Holly Near was performing. At some point she started singing the words, "Why does my love make you uncomfortable? It's love, only love, my love for a woman." And all of a sudden my whole body responded, and I had the thought that my friendship with Grace was more than just friendship. That was the moment of recognition for me. I felt a physical attraction for her that was something more than for a close friend.

We have a calm and steady relationship. It's the way that it ought to be. You depend on each other, love and respect each other.

I had previously been married to a very good man and had a good marriage, but I always considered his career to be more important than mine. I felt that people always identified me through him.

Although each of us has her own strengths, I feel equal when I'm with Grace. Our days aren't fraught with agonizing thoughts, such as "Am I loved? Am I still loved? Are you going to leave me?" We have a calm and steady relationship. It's the way that it ought to be. You depend on each other, love and respect each other. We spend most of our time together. Not many days go by that we don't say, "How lucky we are!"

GRACE: With George and I both being artists, there was some competitiveness in my marriage, too. We always battled over what we jokingly called "equal wall space." Whose paintings were going to hang where? There was only so much wall space.

When I first became friends with Amelia, I didn't think the relationship would be more than a deep friendship. Yet, I quickly realized that this was something very different, that I didn't really understand what was going on between us. I remember once I saw Amelia coming over the hill toward my house. As I watched her I felt something very different about her, but at that time I didn't identify it as a physical attraction or love. I had never had a love relationship with a woman before, but I recognized my feelings for Amelia were very different.

Our relationship is now one of total commitment. It's the best thing that has ever happened to me. I don't really know how to describe the change except that it was a transition from deep friendship to a total love relationship, a full partnership that's deep and profound.

Our relationship is now one of total commitment. It's the best thing that has ever happened to me. I don't really know how to describe the change except that it was a transition from deep friendship to a total love relationship, a full partnership that's deep and profound. Amelia and I have built a home together. We've both put a lot of energy into making it a warm and comfortable place to live. I've always worked in a studio at home, and owning a home together is a very significant thing for me.

I feel strongly about using organic food, so I do the cooking. We shop together. Amelia does the laundry. We have a trainer, and we work out regularly. We put a lot of effort into keeping well and staying physically and mentally active. Illness is something we think about as we get older. We've named each other in our wills and assigned each other medical power of attorney.

Both of my sons have talked with me about my relationship with Amelia. When I told them that we had become committed partners and that we loved each another, they both were very supportive. They've always supported my having a good life. I have five grandchildren, and they all really love Amelia. One of my granddaughters joked, "Should we call Amelia 'Grandpa?'"

AMELIA: We're both close friends with Grace's ex-husband, George, and we've developed friendships with several heterosexual couples over the years. We have more friends than we have time to see. Grace and I enjoy our own company, so we do a lot of things just the two of us together. We're not only supportive of one another in good times, but we take care of each other in bad times. I once got a severe bacterial infection while traveling out of the country and became very, very ill. Grace took charge of my care. I was very ill for three or four months and then had surgery. It took me almost a year to recover, and Grace took great care of me. When Grace had a hip replacement, it was my turn to care for her. We care for each other in sickness and in health.

I have five grandchildren, and they all really love Amelia. One of my granddaughters joked, "Should we call Amelia 'Grandpa?'"

GRACE: Amelia's career has changed since we've been together, and that has been interesting. She took a sabbatical year from her position at the University and decided not to go back. We had been working on our individual art projects together for quite a while, and Amelia decided to take classes where I teach. Family and spouses of faculty get their tuition covered, so we registered as domestic partners to get the benefit. She took both the media program and the fine arts program. Now that we're both artists, our lives are connected even more.

It's wonderful to be with someone who is physically loving and demonstrative. Touching is very important in our relationship. It's beautiful and fulfilling. Even touching in a casual way. We were at a party last evening, and a couple of times we rubbed shoulders. We were aware of each other in a physical way. It doesn't have to manifest in the same way that heterosexual couples think of sexual activity. Loving and lovemaking aren't just about sex. Our culture doesn't understand this well. Our touching is a very caring and authentic thing.

Part of my history included an art exhibit in the late 1960s and early 1970s. It was called "Love Drawings." I realize now that those drawings worked out my feelings that a deep relationship is based on love, not sex. There was a lot of politics around those works, as some saw them as very sexual when they were exhibited. I was always very firm that they were love drawings. That seems consistent with how I still feel.

It's wonderful to be with someone who is physically loving and demonstrative. Touching is very important in our relationship.

Although I'm no longer full-time at the art school, I still teach and mentor art students. Amelia and I teach together sometimes, and that's stimulating and a great deal of fun. Most of my time is spent painting these days. I'm working on a large body of work called "Women in the World: Visionaries and Survivors." I want to show how the world is different because of how women are thinking and living.

AMELIA: Sharing my life with Grace has made me a healthier, stronger, and better person. This second half of our lives is, as the psychologist Carl Jung said, a "moving towards fullness of being." Grace helps me do this. I can trust my heart and soul and body to her, and that's extremely important and comforting.

GRACE: I love what Amelia just said about our relationship, and I'll add this: I've never had so much fun in my life as I've had with Amelia. Although I've slowed up some in these last years, our lives are joyous and rich. I feel safe in our partnership, and that's the best thing anybody could hope to have in her life.

An added comfort in this relationship is that we share expenses equally. Amelia pays for certain things, and I cover my financial responsibilities. At the end of the year we tally up what we've spent, and most of the time it comes out almost equal. The best thing for me about how we run our financial lives is that my partner is extremely responsible. I trust her to pay her bills, and she trusts me. Amelia sometimes worries about, as she puts it, "the economy going south," but if necessary we could move into our little summer place up north and live simply and it would still be a good life.

I believe that people get the love they need at different times in their life and that it often comes from different places and with different persons.

AMELIA: I left the academic world to become a full-time artist. I'm a painter and photographer. We both love to work. We share the same studio so we can see each other when we're working on our art. We get energy from one another. Often we paint from early morning right through the day. It's fun to do this together and very rewarding. And then it's time for tea or wine and cheese, and we share that part of our day as well.

I believe that people get the love they need at different times in their life and that it often comes from different places and with different persons. Now my life and my love are with Grace.

SHARON AND ALEX

Sharon, seventy-two, and Alex, seventy-nine, describe their relationship as being attached yet independent. While many couples I talked with found security and stability in a traditional marriage, some, like Sharon and Alex, have established their togetherness in their own way. I met with them one afternoon at Sharon's comfortable home. They sat close to one another, smiling. I asked them to tell me the story of how they got together. The conversation began with a look back at the final years of their previous marriages.

SHARON: For fourteen years my husband was in ill health with five incurable conditions. Formerly a very vigorous man, he had a heart problem that sent him to the emergency room more than a dozen times, often in the middle of the night: peripheral neuropathy, which caused intense pain in the bottoms of his feet and made it difficult for him to walk; macular degeneration, which eventually led to him being legally blind; Alzheimer's disease; and Parkinson's disease.

Our daughter and her small son lived with us for the final four years, and we all shared in his care at home. I'm certain that the presence of a young child helped Jim maintain his loving connection for so long. Only the final three months of his life did he have to be in a nursing home. He was often "far away," yet he still knew us and was gracious toward us even when he was out of touch with other realities. Alex's wife became very ill and died within two days. He really didn't have a chance to say those last words from the heart, whereas my husband and I had many, many conversations about "last things."

After my husband's death, it took me nearly three years to regain my everyday strength. I never thought about marrying. I didn't even think about dating. Yet I remembered that a few months after my husband died, one of my sons said, "Mom, I want you to be happy. If you meet someone who asks you to go out with him, it's okay. I want you to know that whatever you do, if it makes you happy, that's fine with me. I'll always miss my dad, of course, but I'll support any decision you make and anybody you decide you want to be with."

After my husband's death, it took me nearly three years to regain my everyday strength. I never thought about marrying. I didn't even think about dating.

ALEX: Sharon and I met on a blind date that was actually set up by my brother-in-law. First he called me and said he wanted me to meet a woman who had been a widow for a number of years. I said, okay, that would be fine. He then contacted my son and daughter and Sharon's brother and I don't know who else in each of our families to check if it was all right for us to meet. The way he so carefully set it up was almost Victorian. So Sharon and I met and talked, and then we went on a date, and we got along pretty well, so several dates followed. And that's how it began.

SHARON: One of my fears was that I would hook up with a man whose idea of a good time was to get in an RV and go visit all the relatives. Or who would expect me to redecorate his condo while he went golfing. That was not the kind of relationship that would fit for me. Anyway, I wasn't looking for a man in my life.

Alex didn't remember that we had actually met briefly at a wedding a year after his wife died. That was about three years after my husband died, and neither of us was ready to date at that stage of the game; it was still too raw for both of us. But when I got the call about meeting Alex, after it had been thoroughly checked out and approved by both families as he told you, a little bell went off in my head, and I realized I could go to a movie or to dinner with someone and that didn't mean marriage. I had thought in my head that it wasn't right for me to go on a date unless I was ready to marry again, which I wasn't, and I'm still not interested in marriage. I started to think, "Gee, it would be so nice to have someone to spend some time with—to call and invite me to a meal or a movie." I was ready for some fun.

We've been together four years now, and we've gotten more and more attached to each other, but we don't want to get married. Both of us cherish our independence.

We've been together four years now, and we've gotten more and more attached to each other, but we don't want to get married. Both of us cherish our independence, and we don't want to deal with such decisions as whose house are we going to live in, or what to do about the money, and all that. We feel that marriage wouldn't add any value to our relationship. It wouldn't accomplish anything or give us anything we don't already have with each other.

ALEX: We each have our own homes. I come here to Sharon's house often, and sometimes she comes to my place. We spend the night together a fair amount of the time, and that arrangement works for us. We stay together when we travel to other places and take vacations. As for intimacy—well, I know that young people wonder if old people actually do it. Yes, they do. We both have a significant amount of sexual energy. We've been quite active in that regard. We aren't afraid to show our affection. We often spend nights at each other's homes. We have visitor's rights and visitor's privileges.

SHARON: Alex and I talk extensively about a lot of things, including sexual intimacy. When we were younger, we both believed in waiting until marriage for sex. We were both faithful to our partners, and we still believe that was right. But we also now believe that the commitment we have to this relationship, without marriage, allows for sexual intimacy. We agree that we can practice fidelity in a strong intimate relationship, and this understanding is a fuller expression of the depth of our being together.

I know that young people wonder if old people actually do it. Yes, they do. We both have a significant amount of sexual energy.

Some people don't accept this kind of a relationship. Yesterday I was talking to a couple of "stick-in-the-mud" Lutherans at church. One of them said she thought it was nice that Alex and I were dating and considered it an important relationship. The other one pulled away when I said we weren't planning to marry. Alex and I don't feel we have to marry to serve other people's expectations. I have an adequate income and my house is paid for, so I don't need to marry for financial support. I learned in the fourteen years that I was a caregiver for my husband how to manage everything. I'm a very independent person. Alex, too, is a resourceful person. He's not looking for a woman to pamper him or to take his wife's place, and I'm not looking for him to be what my husband was for me or take his place.

ALEX: Because we each live in our own house, we don't have any situations like some might on how to stack the dishes or fold the laundry. Sharon runs her house as she's used to doing, and I do the same. We come at things in different ways. I analyze things from a scientific background, and Sharon thinks about things in more subjective ways. We're getting used to how differently each of us thinks and approaches things, but we have our own way of analyzing situations and problems. Our brains just function differently. Sometimes Sharon gets impatient with me because I go straight to facts and she sees things from a point of view of empathy. We don't really argue very often. Actually I don't think we ever do. Sometimes we have a disagreement, but we quickly reach a compromise and avoid problems. There are times when one of us has hurt the other, but we've learned to speak about it right away and to work through it as best we can. Most times it is just a misunderstanding, but there have been times when some remark one of us makes has an edge of annoyance or irritation. We both are able to apologize and forgive. We learned this from our long marriages.

We both are able to apologize and forgive. We learned this from our long marriages.

SHARON: When it came time for my family to meet Alex, my son and his wife loved him right away. I know that my son was deeply attached to his dad, and he told me, "I will always miss Dad, but Mom, he's dead and you're alive, and I want you to be happy." My daughter also had very strong feelings for her father. She lived here in the house and helped me care for him during his long illness. In spite of her deep attachment to her dad, I know she tells people that she's glad that I have such a good person for a companion. She's happy for me because she sees me having some of life's joys without the burdens of my husband's long illness.

ALEX: We see each other's families at celebrations and holidays, but we don't make each other's families the focal point of our lives. I'm with my family a lot, but Sharon is with my children and grandchildren only occasionally. The same is true for me on her side. We enjoy each other's families. I have four children and six grandchildren. Sharon has three children and five grandchildren. When we let the families know that we had a serious relationship, the males in the family took the news more comfortably than the females. We thought that the girls probably were thinking of me with their mother, and Sharon with her husband. It took a little longer for them to accept the relationship.

SHARON: As Lutherans, both Alex and I feel we're called to things, and at this time I don't feel called to be a married person. I really don't think either of us wants to give our relationship the test of daily life. I used to worry sometimes that I was just spending time with Alex for my own pleasure and enjoyment. There was a lot in my life that I wouldn't allow myself for a long time. Now I have what I call the privilege of having simple joys. I don't have the feeling anymore of this being a self-serving relationship. Now Alex and I talk every day, and when we feel like going somewhere or doing something we just pick up and go. We both appreciate the spontaneity we have in our relationship.

There was a lot in my life that I wouldn't allow myself for a long time. Now I have what I call the privilege of having simple joys.

ALEX: We enjoy reading poetry to each other. It started early in our relationship one day when Sharon came over to my place feeling quite tender. It was shortly after 9/11, and we were both having feelings of pain and sadness. So I read poetry to her, and she told me it was very healing. We've been reading poetry to each other, not regularly, but often, ever since. Also, we constantly exchange articles and books and things we want the other person to read. And we go to the theater quite often. I hadn't gone to see plays for many years because my wife had a hearing loss and couldn't enjoy doing that, and Sharon's husband had a hearing loss, too. We've extended each other's social life and intellectual life as well.

SHARON: We continue to get to know each other better and explore deeper levels of understanding and sharing. I recall one conversation when I was telling Alex about the struggles I had with my dad, who was not an easy person to be around and to love. He was often unkind to my mother and my brother. Alex asked me if I'd ever forgiven my dad, and I realized I was still holding that resentment. Alex and I grew very close during our discussion about not being able to forgive and the corrosive effect it has on the human spirit, and being a physician he detailed the effects on the body of holding such feelings.

I found it unbelievably wonderful to carry on a sustained conversation with an interesting person. Sometimes I'd sob for the joy of it.

I found it unbelievably wonderful to carry on a sustained conversation with an interesting person. Sometimes I'd sob for the joy of it, because for so many years at the end of his life my husband wasn't able to converse with me. Likewise, because I'd been married to a very thoughtful and loving man, I felt privileged to know Alex, who is loving and thoughtful. And because he had cared for many older people during his years in medicine, he could imagine my situation, and he was willing to let me complete my grieving. In turn, he could talk with me about his losses, and I could help him through his remaining raw grief. We both were surprised that there was still grieving to do, but there was.

As we continue to get to know one another, our separate worlds of experience continue to be a source of enjoyment. I learn from him every day, and he learns from me. We ask one another a lot of questions about our worlds, our assumptions, our practices, our relationships, so both of us have become more flexible in our thinking and feeling. Recently he said to me, "I want you to know that one thing I appreciate about you is that you find so much joy in your work. That comes through very clearly about you." And my work is very important to me.

Early on, Alex and I had a conversation about some of our values. We talked a lot about what we do out in the world to help in many situations, not to make a big impact, but to do things for others that expose us to more than the world that we personally know. His interests are very different from some doctors I know who live only in their world of upper-class patients. Because of Alex's work at the University and his work as a program director for residencies in family medicine, he's worked in many clinics that care for underserved people. Service is an important value we share.

As we continue to get to know one another, our separate worlds of experience continue to be a source of enjoyment. I learn from him every day, and he learns from me.

ALEX: When Sharon and I got to know each other, she told me that she secretly dreaded I would be the stereotype of an upper-middle-class doctor who didn't see beyond the patient that could easily afford medical care. But we both believe strongly in working to help others. I've volunteered in many situations where medical help was needed and have worked in several clinics around the city that serve underserved populations. I've also gone to Africa to help people who needed medical care.

As a retired physician I've also been consulting recently on medical education and have also been doing some legal work as a plaintiff witness in medical cases. But my work doesn't take all my time, by any means. I have plenty of time for hobbies and things I enjoy. In the summertime, I work a lot in my garden; I'm a master gardener.

SHARON: I've worked for several years with a youth development organization on many national research projects in many different environments. I've worked all over the country helping organizations and communities support young people in their development. Alex and I both had adults in our lives who encouraged us and moved us along. We each came from families that really valued education, who helped us as we went through school and decided what to do with our lives. We both had what we think all children need. About two-thirds of American kids feel they have no role models—adults who care, schools that really care.

We both believe strongly in working to help others.

Providing this kind of help and support to kids is a passion of mine, not just in my work but also in my own life.

I love my work, and Alex enjoys the projects he takes on as well, but, like Alex, I don't have to work all the time. I garden, I take time for exercise, and I take time to be with friends. So many things that weren't part of my life before have become important to me now. Alex and I share the values of staying alive intellectually, talking with interesting people, and doing volunteer work. I have some friends who are busy, busy, busy all the time. I don't want to live that way. I want time to take care of my health and do the things I enjoy besides my work.

We've traveled together quite a bit. Alex loves history and has read extensively, so when we visit places in another country, it's like having my own private audiotape walking next to me. He knows all about the history and the architecture and the culture of many countries. I'm always busy with my work until we leave on a trip, so Alex does the research and teaches me along the way. We have the privilege of personal enrichment and the satisfaction of civic engagement.

Neither of us is that interested in eating out at restaurants. And neither of us likes to eat alone. Sometimes we get together at one of our houses just to have tea and toast. We like that because we enjoy sitting across the table from each other and having long conversations. We don't need the clattering of dishes, and we don't have to get up and leave in the middle of a conversation—and we don't need to spend a lot of money and eat too much food.

I have some friends who are busy, busy, busy all the time. I don't want to live that way. I want time to take care of my health and do the things I enjoy besides my work.

We also have similar values in terms of money. We talked early in our being together about money and decided that when we go out, the one that invites, pays. If I invite Alex to a concert, I pay, and if he suggests we go out, then he pays. When we were on trips together, we used to add the costs up and divide them at the end of the trip, but that got cumbersome. Now we keep track as we go along, and it's fifty-fifty. We haven't had any problems at all about money.

ALEX: We very carefully plan our trips so that we go someplace that we both really feel strongly about seeing. Before we had a relationship, I went to see the tulips in the Netherlands and also went to the Amazon and Africa. None of those places interest Sharon, so I'm glad I took those trips before Sharon and I traveled together. We've gone on two trips to Italy together and once to France as well.

SHARON: In the past I've led an overwhelmed life. My tendency is to make my life too full. One of the things I appreciate about Alex is that he challenges that. And when Alex and I have talked about how much I'm always taking on, I've come to realize that there are many things I just don't want to do again. I loved the work when I did it. Now I don't want to do that kind of work anymore. I've started to clear out my files, and I filled twelve bags to throw away. I've turned down some consulting jobs, and I'm changing my lifestyle. My whole body says, "I don't want to do that again." I'm becoming very selective about the commitments I make.

Although I'm quite healthy, when I turned seventy-one I realized that it was important that Alex and I talk about changes in health and the challenges that could come with our later years. I just had a biopsy. I think everything is fine. My surgeon thinks I'm okay, but you never know about these things. We discussed what our expectations are of each other in the face of serious illness. I had many years of being a caregiver for my husband. Alex's wife died very suddenly. We realize that at some time, one of us will lose the other, but we don't know what health challenges we'll face in between. We've agreed— given that the nature of our relationship is a commitment, not a marriage—that each of us is responsible for his or her own care. I do not expect Alex, even though he's a doctor, to take over my care.

Although I'm quite healthy, when I turned seventy-one I realized that it was important that Alex and I talk about changes in health and the challenges that could come in our later years.

Because we love each other and will have had this long relationship, we can be there to be helpful and comforting. Alex is a very thoughtful, tender, and attentive person when I don't feel well or when I'm tired or too used up to follow through on a plan we might have made. I have total confidence in Alex to be thoughtful and undemanding. I know, however, that I couldn't move in for months at a time and be Alex's full-time caregiver, and I would not expect that of him. When you're not married and don't have legal rights, it's tough dealing with medical emergencies or making medical decisions. I don't want to step into his children's territory. My power of attorney is with my children as far as health care directives, my will, and whatever major decisions have to be made. I would never expect Alex to have to make major decisions for me; that will be my children's responsibility. Alex has taken care of these things for himself in the same manner.

When we came into each other's lives, we discovered that our past histories were always coming up. Alex was married forty-two years; I was married forty-one. There's a whole history of careers, of children, of sorrows and joys, of disappointments and regrets. We discovered that if you live too much in the past, then you aren't living in the present. We soon realized that our early conversations weren't helping us to write our story. The past is not our story. We often make references to the past, but I've made a decision to live in the moment.

When you're not married and don't have legal rights, it's tough dealing with medical emergencies or making medical decisions.

I'll tell you a story that brought that change about. Alex and I went on a drive in the country to see the changing of the leaves. As we were driving over familiar territory, I looked at a bright red sumac and immediately started to cry. I was remembering the last time I took my husband on the same drive. He was legally blind, and he couldn't see color. Yet he said, "Look at the brilliant sumac." I replied to him something about his not being able to see color, and he replied, "I see the sumac as shiny black, and my memory tells me what color it is." That was what brought on the tears. But I made a decision not verbalize what I was thinking. I made a conscious decision to stay in the moment with Alex and not keep going back to the past and saying things like, "I remember when we bought apples there, and stopped there, and walked there." You can go on forever about the past. We often make references to what our lives were, but we consciously work on staying in the present.

Things are very different in a new relationship. After being married to the same person for over forty years, learning to accept another person who is very different is a challenge. If you love a person, you can learn to love that difference. You learn to let some things go, realizing that you can't change old habits. Sometimes I just want to say, "That isn't the way to do that." But why bother? It's not that important. Maybe this is easier for me to say because we're not together all the time and we have our separate time in our own houses. We diffuse a lot of these kinds of things because we're not together all the time.

Things are very different in a new relationship. After being married to the same person for over forty years, learning to accept another person who is very different is a challenge.

A beautiful thing in our relationship happened recently when one of Alex's daughters was married. The reception was at his house, and Alex asked me if I would please join him for the wedding and the other events surrounding the celebration of the marriage. I was hesitant because I didn't want to be an intruder. I knew the family would miss their mother. Alex asked me several times to please join the wedding party. I told him that I wouldn't stand by him after the ceremony because people would want to talk about his wife, the children's mother, and how sad it was that she didn't live to see her daughter married and how much they missed her. When the evening was over I told Alex that I thought I'd leave. There were still things going on, but I felt it was time for me go. Then in the midst of his family Alex turned to me and said, "Thank you, darling, for coming. I appreciate it so much." And he kissed me and said goodbye. That sweet gesture meant a great deal to me. He wouldn't have had to do that thoughtful, tender thing. Those little things mean a great deal.

CAROL AND CARL

It was a shared love for chamber music that brought Carol and Carl together. They've since discovered that opera, theater, museums, and art exhibitions are also more interesting and fun when attended with another person. Carol is seventy-three; Carl is eighty-one. They've been married for seven years. "There seem to be a lot of older couples in new relationships," Carol told me. "This summer we're attending the wedding of two 'almost octogenarians.'"

CAROL: I had lived a busy and interesting life before my divorce, and I wanted to maintain that lifestyle. I started collecting flyers and information on all the places I wanted to travel and the many new things I wanted to experience. My collection included lectures, hikes, and cultural events that were available in New York City, where I live. I also looked for ways to meet people. One of the venues I explored was the Classical Music Lovers Exchange.

All the people listed in the Exchange had written a twenty-five-word description of themselves. Carl's said that he'd had a very long marriage, was recently widowed, and was only looking for a friend. I thought, "Okay—male friend. That would be fine." So I called him, and that's how we met.

CARL: I was really lying to myself about only wanting a friend. After meeting Carol, I quickly realized that I wanted more than just friendship. I told Carol on our second date that I loved her. When my wife died, we had been married forty-eight years. Ten years before she died she was already ill with diabetes, Parkinson's, and heart problems. One day she wrote a letter and told me it was to be opened when she died. I opened the letter after she passed away and found that she had made two requests. The first was that when our three children came to visit we were all to have a Chinese meal on her, and she specified the restaurant. We had long before given up Chinese restaurants because the sodium in the food

I was really lying to myself about only wanting a friend. After meeting Carol, I quickly realized that I wanted more than just friendship.

was bad for her health. The second request was that I was to mourn her for a week and then go out and find somebody to be my partner. That was actually a release. The message was simple. "I'm dead, you're alive, so live."

CAROL: On our first date we went to the Metropolitan Museum. That's the kind of thing we enjoy doing together— museums, opera, concerts, theatre, art exhibits. Carl is highly intelligent, with good values and a good sense of humor. He enjoys the culture of New York City and also has a great appreciation of nature. We love New York and wouldn't live anywhere else. Also, my three children and grandchildren live here, and two of Carl's three children live here, too. Once we got together it wasn't too long before we were living together, and then we decided to get married and make it official. My children were very happy for me. I had been alone for a long time, and now they could worry about me less.

Carl and I made a prenuptial agreement. We wanted to ensure that our premarital assets would go to our children and grandchildren. Each month we add up all the checks and charges and, except for personal items like a gift one may have purchased for other, divide everything in half.

CARL: I moved into Carol's home, and the biggest challenge in making that move was to get rid of five thousand books. I was able to find a library that would take them. I kept probably a thousand of my books and moved them into Carol's home. I got rid of most of my furniture. It wasn't worth much unless you consider a fifty-year-old chest of drawers an antique. I wasn't attached to most of the furniture. I brought a couple of pieces with me, but that's about all. Two of my three children expressed warm feelings for my getting married. One of my daughters had reservations. She was reluctant and didn't attend the wedding. It was unclear to me why, as she never actually gave me a reason. One of the things I learned at an early age was the difference between when I had a problem and somebody else had the problem. In this case, it's her problem, not mine.

Carl and I made a prenuptial agreement. We wanted to ensure that our premarital assets would go to our children and grandchildren.

Carol is younger than I am. She's seventy-three and in very good health. I'm eighty years old. I've had double bypass and gall bladder surgery. And I had a fall while I was in the hospital for the gall bladder surgery, which resulted in two fractured vertebrae, so now I walk very slowly with a cane. Otherwise, I'm in good health.

We've always traveled a lot, but now that I'm afraid each trip might be our last, we're traveling even more. I'm trying to squeeze it all in. We went on a scheduled trip to Sicily even though I was in pain from having just had the gall bladder surgery. Carol packed an extra suitcase with all the things necessary to dress an open wound. She had experience as a caregiver in her first marriage. She nursed her husband through two heart attacks and various other illnesses.

CAROL: My vision of retirement was to be able to contribute something to society, keep myself in good shape physically, and do something for myself—things that I enjoy doing. After I retired, I went back to school and got a degree in a new field. I now have a late-life career as a genetic counselor in a prenatal clinic. My friends are doing interesting things as well. They don't fit that negative stereotype of aging of sitting in a rocking chair and not doing much. They read, they have ideas and projects, and they contribute to society.

As you age, every aspect of intimacy remains important—holding hands and cuddling, as well as actual sex. It's an important dimension of life, and we joyfully partake in it.

While I have a very fine memory for early events, I sometimes have problems with names and more recent events. Still, I find that I'm able to learn new things. Of course, some older people do have dementia, and this fact can reinforce negative stereotypes of the elderly. People also make negative generalizations about intimacy and older persons. For many years I was a biology teacher. As part of my course I taught reproduction, and I always stressed that sexuality was a part of mature life. Some young people fear that life ends at age thirty-five. Of course, they're wrong. As you age, every aspect of intimacy remains important—holding hands and cuddling, as well as actual sex. It's an important dimension of life, and we joyfully partake in it.

CARL: Our relationship has been growing deeper on its own. You don't plan a relationship; you just live it. One thing I've learned is that many things in life are trivial. There's no point in getting upset about the little things in a personal relationship. Yet I see this happen a lot. People argue about trivial things, small stuff. If you're on the same frequency, if you have the same values—a love for the same kinds of things—then the flaws and small differences really don't matter. If I get annoyed at some trivial thing, I tell myself to laugh instead of criticize. But Carol will tell you that we do sometimes argue about the little things—for example, clutter in the house. I let things pile up, but I know where they are. I have a very orderly, disorderly desk. But Carol doesn't like my clutter.

You don't plan a relationship; you just live it.

Our families have merged in many ways. Carol has four children and five grandchildren, and the youngest ones I've enjoyed immensely. Two of the girls, a three-year-old and a six-year-old, are charmers. It's been a joy to be with them. Mine are older; they're teenagers.

CAROL: Many of Carl's friends have died, so when we came together he acquired all my friends, and this contributes to our social life. We see our friends often, and they're an important part of our lives. We're in a very interesting book club group. Reading the same books is something we enjoy doing very much. We have a small cabin in the Adirondacks, where I taught Carl how to paddle a canoe. We have all the culture New York has to offer and the outdoors of our small place on a lake. It's a good life.

ESTELLE AND NORM

*"I'm seventy-eight now," Norm told me. "Estelle is two years younger. We're living together in two houses ... one at a time. We live mostly in Estelle's in the summer because her place is on the river. We're at my place in the winter."
Estelle and Norm have no plans to sell either of their homes. Each place is beautifully furnished with art, antiques, and every appliance necessary for comfortable living. Norm's wife died after fifty years of marriage. Estelle's been married twice. Her first husband died when she was thirty-seven, leaving her to care for their four children alone. Her second husband died several years before she met Norm.*

NORM: I first met Estelle about four years ago. My wife had died two years earlier. I was in a coffee shop with three or four of my friends. It was taking us quite a while for us to finish the Sunday crossword puzzle in the *New York Times*. One of the fellows left the table and wandered around a bit. He came back very excited and said, "There's a woman over there doing the Sunday crossword by herself—in ink!" Now that's an example of real self-confidence, I thought, so I went over to her table, and we talked briefly. Then, much later, I saw her again in that same coffee shop, and she came over to me and said, "Hello, Norm. How are you? And how's your wife doing?" I told her that my wife had died. Then I asked her, "How's your husband?" And she told me that he had passed away recently. So I said, "Can I call you?" What attracted me to her was her brightness and vivacity. We met for a coffee date and talked and talked. I guess I was no longer interested in being alone.

When we had our first coffee date and were just getting to know each other, I pulled out a postcard about a play I thought she might like to go see with me. She said, "I'll put the card on my refrigerator next to the Archbishop of Canterbury." I thought it was a little strange if she was cutting out pictures of the Archbishop and mounting them on her refrigerator. But later, when she invited me to her house, I saw that she was referring to a photograph of herself with the Archbishop of Canterbury. Now when she casually says that she probably knows everyone in the world, I'm inclined to believe her.

My friend came back very excited and said, "There's a woman over there doing the Sunday crossword by herself—in ink!" Now that's an example of real self-confidence, I thought.

This first date was in February, near Valentine's Day, and I was dating another woman at that time. I wanted to send something to this woman and to Estelle, too. I got two very noncommittal Valentine cards and mailed them. The other woman thanked me, but Estelle gave me a hug. I had never been a hugger, and my wife hadn't been particularly demonstrative. After her death, many people gave me a big hug to express their sympathy. That was new to me, and I thought, "Boy, this is nice."

So Estelle and I started seeing each other, and after about ten days we just stayed together. There was no formal decision, really. She was working during the daytime, and I was busy, too, and we were together every night. We both just wanted to keep that routine going.

ESTELLE: Norm's house is on the same country road as my son's home. One day at a neighborhood coffee klatsch a woman said, "Norm has a new girlfriend." At which point my son's wife said, "Yeah, we know. It's my mother-in-law." It was amusing, and we all joke about it now. It never really occurred to me to care what my children or the neighbors thought. Why would I, in my seventies, give a hoot about what people think? It did happen rather quickly, I'll admit. Maybe because of our ages we just got there faster. My family would never have the temerity to confront me about my behavior.

Why would I, in my seventies, give a hoot about what people think?

NORM: When I told my son about Estelle and that she had lost two husbands, he asked questions like, "What did she poison them with?" and "Are you sure you're going to be okay?" Not to worry, I told him. Her first husband was killed in a helicopter accident and the other died of a stroke.

ESTELLE: The whole thing was incredibly surprising and swift. Was I looking for a mate? Good Lord, no! But Norman is the most romantic man I've ever known. He sends cards and leaves sweet notes—things like that. I thought these sorts of things only happened in novels and movies. I didn't know people really did them.

As for feeling married to Norm … we have a bond that is more spiritual than legal. We've had time in our lives to make mistakes and learn, and we're very clear now on what we want at this time of our lives.

NORM: I felt serious about this relationship quickly, and I came to love Estelle very much. She didn't express any interest in getting married, but I was willing to if she wanted to. Estelle has a longtime friend who is an Episcopal priest living in the south of France. A couple of years ago we went to France to visit, and to my surprise, but certainly not my displeasure, Estelle asked the priest if she would do something a bit out of the ordinary. Estelle wanted to have a ceremony—not a marriage, but something like a marriage. The priest agreed, and we planned the event. It included traditional vows, but we changed one phrase, from "lawfully wedded wife (or husband)" to "spiritually wedded wife (or husband)." Our relationship has a depth and intensity that I can hardly believe. We have no official marriage license, but we feel and act married.

We have a bond that is more spiritual than legal. We've had time in our lives to make mistakes and learn, and we're very clear now on what we want at this time of our lives.

ESTELLE: We have a strong intellectual component in our relationship and a wonderful companionship. We both respond to intelligent and insightful people who have had interesting life experiences. We both love theater, music, and art. And we have ordered, warm, welcoming households. I want a supportive environment for my family when they come to visit, and I'm very willing to give that to his family also.

NORM: We plan to keep both of our houses. Estelle's place is five minutes closer to town than mine, and sometimes it's just easier to stop and stay at the first house we come to if we're out late in the evening, especially in the winter. I like my house and wish we'd spend more time there. We entertain mainly at my house. Sometimes for fund-raisers we donate a brunch and a tour of my art collection. Estelle jokes that her house doesn't have enough wall space and room for art, and mine doesn't have enough closets for her clothes. We each keep up the expenses on our own house. Purchases like theater tickets, gasoline, and groceries we put on one credit card, and we each pay half when the bill when it comes. We don't keep exact track of who spends what when we use cash, but I think we're both comfortable that it seems fair.

ESTELLE: It had been a long time since physical intimacy had been a part of my life. My husband had had a long physical decline, and I'd really gotten away from that kind of thing. The common joke is that children of any age don't want to think of their parents knowing anything about sex or doing anything sexual. Somehow they don't associate it with their being here. Well, I think sex is great! I find there's a frivolity about sex at our stage of life. It unfolds the way it ought to. There's no pretense. What you see is what you get. There's nothing to hide by the time you get to your seventies. I'm very relaxed about touching and nudity. I'm not upset about these things like many in my generation were conditioned to be. We really enjoy sex in a relaxed fashion and find sexual expression in a lot of ways. We just need a cool, comfortable place to be relaxed and no pressure to get anywhere.

I find there's a frivolity about sex at our stage of life. It unfolds the way it ought to. There's no pretense. What you see is what you get. There's nothing to hide by the time you get to your seventies.

NORM: Our cuddling is as important as anything. And we're compatible in many ways other than just physically. We like the same kinds of food, restaurants, plays, movies, people. If

I'm cooking, for example, but I'm not doing it the way that Estelle would, she just leaves the kitchen. I do the same when the situation is reversed. We don't get into hassles about little things. We don't often have differences of opinion on things. At this point in our lives we bring a lot of experience and judgment about what is worth fighting about and what isn't. And if we have a difference of opinion, we never bury it, let it fester, or hold grudges like we may have done when we were younger. Maybe that's the most important lesson I've learned in life. We really never fight about anything. What's there to fight about?

ESTELLE: But we do have one small issue, and that's clutter. I have a need for order and neatness. I don't even have to have cleanliness just as long as things are in order. It gives me the illusion that I have order and neatness in my life, though I know in reality I don't always have that. Order gives me comfort. I guess that's why I cling to it. I have a filing system so I know where all the stuff I want is. If a newspaper or magazine isn't read by a certain time, it's gone. I'm quite disciplined about this because it's so much easier now to replace these things at the library or online. If you miss an article in last week's paper, you can easily get it. We get four newspapers a day, and they pile up fast. Norm says he's okay now with me snatching newspapers out from under him. When we're at Norm's house, he handles his clutter his way. If there's a closed door, it's understood you don't open it. I've been known to get angry about his clutter. But Norm says it's a nice, neat, civilized, focused anger that he can understand.

At this point in our lives we bring a lot of experience and judgment about what is worth fighting about and what isn't. And if we have a difference of opinion, we never bury it, let it fester, or hold grudges like we may have done when we were younger.

NORM: We've had some health issues. Some months after my wife died, I developed a pain in my shoulder that wouldn't go away. One morning I woke up because of the pain and went to the emergency room. I know now it was a heart attack and that I had severe hardening of the arteries. Anyway, I came out of that, went through heart rehab, and at this time everything seems fine. In fact, Estelle and I went to Peru a couple of years ago and climbed Machu Picchu, which is more steps than I had ever seen in my life, and I did okay. I actually consider myself pretty healthy, but I do have type 2 diabetes, so I take medication daily and check my blood sugar regularly.

ESTELLE: We were supposed to be in France right now, doing nothing but relaxing and enjoying ourselves. At the last minute we had to cancel the trip. I wasn't feeling very good—a little nauseated—and food didn't taste very good. I'd been diagnosed a while ago with diverticulitis, and when something like this happens I just put myself on a liquid diet and everything resolves itself. But this time the diet didn't work, so I finally went to the doctor. I probably should have gone in a week earlier. The doctor did some x-rays and detected a mass in the colon. To make a short story long, after about ten days of diagnostics I got into a crisis when the thing burst and my colon became infected.

Norm is wonderful in supporting me not only physically, but psychologically and emotionally. He's really there for me.

Thankfully, they never found any cancer, but they did a colostomy, and now I'm healing. In a couple of months they'll reconnect the plumbing and put me back together again. For now, my personal miracle is Norm. You'd think he'd been dressing raw, open wounds in the abdomen for years, the way he launched into all this. I don't think a lot of men could handle this kind of caretaking responsibility the way he has. He said that he saw the nurses do it, so he just did what they did. He's wonderful in supporting me not only physically, but psychologically and emotionally. He's really there for me.

Norm takes good care of himself as well as me. He's really conscious of the amount of walking he does in a day. He usually parks on one end of town and walks to all his appointments and on all his errands. I haven't been as conscientious as Norm, but after I recover fully from the surgery, which has been a temporary setback, I'm definitely going to start some kind of structured exercise to get my stamina back. I know it's too easy to let your health slip, so I'm really going to work at it.

It brought me up short when I became ill. I hated being ill because for the first time in my life I was out of control. Getting sick has really been an eye-opener for me. It's made me realize I can't put off things that need to be done. It doesn't really matter what age you're at or whether you're

It doesn't really matter what age you're at or whether you're healthy, you should take care of important matters concerning how things should be after your death.

healthy, you should take care of important matters concerning how things should be after your death. My mother thought she had made specific bequests. She'd say to a grandchild, "I want you to have great-grandfather's watch," but she never put these things in writing. And that was sad and heartbreaking as it turned out. You are more in control of your life when you take care of these things. It's easier for me than for some because I always have to be in control. I'd been thinking about personal assets and things like that for quite a long time, but my current illness has been an extra motivation. For example, this house—I'd hate to see it go out of the family. I've taken care of things in my will, but I haven't gone into specifics on the house. There are other loose ends to tie up, and I'm taking the time to do that.

NORM: Both of our houses essentially function on one floor. So we each could accommodate home health care needs when and if it's necessary. Estelle actually had her house adapted with grab bars and railings for her husband after he had his first stroke. Each of our houses can accommodate a walker or a wheelchair if necessary. I suppose we'd defer to the house of the one who could manage alone. We can't really predict what our needs are going to be in the future, but I think both houses can comfortably accommodate a live-in helper if necessary. But for now, Estelle's niece calls us "unmedicated hyperactives."

We can't really predict what our needs are going to be in the future, but I think both houses can comfortably accommodate a live-in helper if necessary. But for now, Estelle's niece calls us "unmedicated hyperactives."

ESTELLE: At this time in our lives we have the time, energy, and resources to take on projects in our community. The issue of community development is our current passion. We're always planting and growing some new idea or project. As fulfilling as just having each other is, and as lucky as we would be if we just had that, what is so exciting for us is having this common interest in societal goals. It isn't just the intellectual connection and our concern for the community, it's an attitude. We both have a readiness to be involved in whatever community needs might present themselves. Doing these kinds of things together enriches our social relationships, the health of the community we live in, and the life that we're building together.

DONNA AND ANDY

Donna and Andy, like some other couples in this book, had a romantic relationship when they were young, then were separated for many years, before reconnecting in their later years. Andy is seventy; Donna is sixty-four. They both work full-time. Andy is an architect, and Donna holds down a demanding position as the head of a national arts organization. "I plan to change my work pattern soon," she said. "I want more hands on with people and less administration." Donna and Andy have learned a lot about themselves over the years, and they're still learning new things in their mature years.

ANDY: Many years ago I saw Donna at a dance concert at college. She was in the back of the group on stage dancing, and that was it, she was all I could see after that. I said to myself, "I'm going to find out who she is." It didn't take long before we were quite serious about each other.

When I graduated college, I wanted Donna to move in with me, but her mother wouldn't let her. She insisted Donna stay in school and study to become a doctor and put dance and theater out of her mind. Her mother was strong and insistent. I was twenty-two, but Donna was only sixteen and not really ready to get married. So I moved from Brooklyn into New York City and soon met someone else. I got married quickly, and we had a son, who is now twenty-eight.

DONNA: I was sixteen and a freshman in college when I met Andy. He was a fabulous dance partner. I fell in love with him back then; he was my first love. Our time together was magic. I grew up quickly. I didn't go to medical school like my mother wanted, but I did stay in college. Andy remained my friend and kept encouraging me to do what I loved, and I became a dancer and a choreographer. I used to be a professional modern dancer, now I dance for my own pleasure. Anyway, I eventually married and had a son, who is now twenty-nine. I was married for thirteen years and then divorced.

I was sixteen and a freshman in college when I met Andy.... I fell in love with him back then; he was my first love.

The man I married was very political. It was the 1960s, and we were both into radical politics. I was in a street theater company, and he was teaching at a community college. We were involved with organizing groups that protested against the war in Vietnam. We did well together on that level but not much else. We had a son and stayed married ten years. I came to my independence through the women's movement. It gave me support for divorcing my husband. We shared many values, and a child as well, but he was not my soul mate, and I came to have no commitment to being married.

One day I found Andy sitting on my front step. He had heard I was divorced and had tracked me down. That was twenty-two years ago, when I was forty-one. Within a couple of weeks of our reconnecting, we took a trip to Europe and made a plan to live together, but it didn't work out. My son was young, and there was a lot of competition for my attention. I felt I had to make a choice. Andy's son wasn't comfortable with the relationship, either. Andy and I terminated our relationship, and I focused on raising my son. I really loved Andy, but it took me four or five years to figure out that I needed him in my life to make me happy. By then my son was in college and Andy's son was grown up as well. Andy now has a good relationship with my son, and I have a comfortable relationship with his son, too.

I don't need to be married. I love being with Andy. We're partners, I know that, so I don't know what the advantage would be to be married. My ninety-three-year-old mother talks to me as if I'm the most sinful woman on earth. She wants to say to her friends that Andy is her son-in-law. I come from a traditional home, and my mother is what we used to call in the women's movement "male-identified." She has traditional values, she'd prefer we were married, but she's come to accept my choice of not being married. She also understands that Andy is my life partner and has my total commitment.

I don't need to be married.... We're partners, I know that, so I don't know what the advantage would be to be married.

I'm not a jealous person. If I'm jealous of anything, it's my own time. Andy has always let me spend time the way I need to, so the time we spend together I value very much. And the time we spend apart I also value very much. Andy is an architect, and I'm the executive director of a national organization. We do our own things. Andy is very understanding of my professional commitments. He truly doesn't resent my travel and other professional responsibilities. We have a deep respect for what each of us feels we have to do on our own.

It sounds like we spend a lot of time apart, but that isn't true. We're together a great deal. When I'm not traveling or working, we're constantly together. We live together, but we have two houses. My place is where we live during the week—our day-to-day house. We stay in my apartment most of the time because it's very close to the nursing facility where my mother resides, and we're her primary caregivers. Andy's home is the weekend house—our "get-away" home—though he goes there every day, since his house doubles as his architecture office.

ANDY: I worked for the city for about ten years as a project architect. Now I'm back on my own, and I love it. I have a very young partner who loves the work, and I'm his mentor. It's fun to pass on the knowledge I have from the class of 1962 to the class of 2002. With him in the office I can take the day off and say, "I'm with Donna. I'm not coming in today."

When Donna and I got back together after twenty years, we realized immediately that things in our physical relationship hadn't changed…. We're both very sensual people.

When Donna and I got back together after twenty years, we realized immediately that things in our physical relationship hadn't changed. We always had high energy in our relationship. I know every wrinkle, every spot on her body. We're both very sensual people. Our physical desire for each other was always there. We love to be together.

DONNA: When we were young, we were passionate and always ready to have sex—anywhere, any time of day or night. Our relationship has always been passionately sexual. We've always been very responsive to one another. I don't know many couples that speak about their loving like that.

We've always had an amazing chemistry for each other. It feels like a very special gift. We are always touching. Our physical relationship, our lovemaking, has always been sacred territory. No arguments, no differences, nothing interferes with our bedroom life. It's really extraordinary.

In the beginning, when we were younger, we made love all night. Now, in our sixties, we laugh a lot and make adjustments. Over the years we've changed. We've slowed down some. It takes longer; it takes patience and gentle caring. We've always been able to talk to each other about making love. We label what we do now "practice sessions." Our rhythms are different. Now it takes us much longer. We do more foreplay, and it's a lot more fun! It's very relaxed. We can talk together about what gives us pleasure, what we want more of or less of. This is important to both of us. This part of our lives is very special.

In the beginning, when we were younger, we made love all night. Now, in our sixties, we laugh a lot and make adjustments.

Do we have disagreements? Well, I raise my voice when I'm angry about something. I actually like to express myself when I'm angry—it feels good. Yet I think that growing older brings us to a place of accepting and accommodating. I'm far more understanding now of the differences between Andy and me. Things that used to upset me—Andy's longwindedness, his not being clear, his tendency to put the responsibility on me for things that affect us both—I'm no longer reacting to.

ANDY: In my marriage it was quite the opposite. If anybody screamed or cursed, it was me. I criticized too much. My behavior led to more problems, so I don't do that at all in my relationship with Donna. It's a non-issue with us. I've totally changed my behavior. Somehow we've managed to divide up chores, the business of living, cooking, cleaning, shopping, and if Donna does things differently than I would, it doesn't bother me. I've learned that you can't change people by yelling. I've learned to pick my battles. This really helps in loving relationships. We never go to bed mad. Our bed is a sacred space.

DONNA: One time many years ago when I was really sick and had a series of operations, Andy's attempt to advocate for me with the medical system made him impatient, and he yelled and demanded. He's not a good negotiator, and I learned from that. When I had surgery another time, I set up a schedule of other people to handle the medical pieces of the situation. I wish Andy was more patient, but that's not one of his attributes. He is there physically, but he doesn't do well in negotiations with the hospital staff.

We never go to bed mad.
Our bed is a sacred space.

ANDY: When Susan had her hysterectomy, I panicked and wasn't there for her. It took a long time to heal our relationship, to rebuild the trust. I guess I've just had too many bad experiences in hospitals— too many people I love have died—and I get anxious in hospitals. I'm better now, as I understand that not everyone who goes to a hospital dies. I'm not as fearful of losing her, and that anxiety I used to get when I couldn't handle the situation doesn't happen anymore. Donna got the brunt of my hysterical reaction in those early years before I learned to handle it.

DONNA: As for other parts of our relationship, we've worked out our finances in a way that's very comfortable for us. I work, so I have a regular income. I shop for food and pay the apartment expenses, and Andy pays for meals when we go out and covers the bills on his place. It just works out, and we're comfortable with that. When we travel, one of us will pay the airfare, the other will cover the hotel. It's not an issue. There's reciprocity, fairness, and consideration on both our parts. We're now in the process of figuring out exactly what we're going to need to live on and if our expenses will be comfortably covered by pensions and Social Security or by renting out one of our living spaces. It has been important to each of us until now to maintain our independence, but this hasn't been financially smart. Now we'll plan to have one house, one car, one telephone. We'll simplify, and things will cost far less. We're paying attention to how we can have the best quality of life in retirement. Two can live more cheaply than one, and it's time to recognize this.

We've lived in lots of different places over our lives together, and now we're going to create another place to live that will be senior oriented. Originally we thought we would retire to the wonderful house that Andy designed and built a number of years ago not far from the apartment where we live during the week. But in the past few months we've decided that this home, while very beautiful, isn't age appropriate. To begin with, you have to be young and agile to climb up and down spiral staircases. I'm starting to get an arthritic neck and hip, and I'm not looking forward to running up and down stairs. So we're focusing on universal design and accessible living. I work in the field of aging so I understand universal design. I know about the kind of house that can accommodate an aging body.

We've worked out our finances in a way that's very comfortable for us.... There's reciprocity, fairness, and consideration on both our parts.

We've changed how we live in many ways, and this has changed our perception of what we need in the place where we live as we age. The type of kitchen we need as we're approaching seventy is quite different from the one we needed when we were forty and having parties and constant company. So as we both slow down from the business of day-to-day work we're thinking about what kind of spaces we want in our lives. I know I want an art studio. I've been helping other people create, and now I want to go back to my own creating, so I need the space. I know we want a yard. I've lived in an apartment my whole life and never had a yard.

ANDY: I know we need a space to read comfortably. We need a sleeping area that can maintain an appropriate temperature, a place to exercise, an area for a garden, studio space for both of us, an area to entertain friends, a guest room—and everything accessible without stairs. We're talking about putting in an elevator into our present place while we're planning the new home. Donna's knees hurt when she walks up stairs, and I may be required to have knee surgery soon, so stairs just don't work for us anymore. Neither of us has a garage, and I'm tired of struggling to find a parking space. And there's pilfering and burglary and parking regulations. We'll have a garage for sure. And we no longer need to live near schools or be concerned about things that raising a family requires. Both of our places are in Brooklyn, and we want to stay in this area. It's important to both of us to be close to New York City. We love New York and have a passion for its people and politics. The energy of New York suits us.

Things are changing for us physically…. Thinking about what is really important for this third age, this last phase of our lives, has been a high priority for me.

DONNA: Things are changing for us physically. In the last year we've both had major medical issues. I fell and had a concussion and have not yet fully recovered. Thinking about what is really important for this third age, this last phase of our lives, has been a high priority for me. A year ago I wouldn't have thought like this, but now I can't wait to focus on something other than being an administrator of a large organization. I'm a very work-oriented person, but I realize that when I retire I'll be doing tasks that will feed my own creative and reflective soul, and I can't wait for that. I'd like to be the voice of history in the classroom as a storyteller. There are so many stories to be told, and the kids today have no idea. In fact, I'd love to be a part of the aging programs I've created in my organization. Bringing history to life for young people by sharing my personal stories and the experiences of my generation would be an exciting and, I believe, important challenge.

ANDY: As busy as we still are, we've spent more time this past year seeing friends and spending time with people we care about. We're all at the stage of life when we're starting to retire and change our pace. Even the busiest of our friends who work seven days a week and evenings too—very task-oriented people—are starting to want other things besides constant work.

I see that the clock is running. If we don't get our plans together while we're in reasonable health, then all of our fantasies will be out the window.

The challenge for me now is to do something for us. I see that the clock is running. If we don't get our plans together while we're in reasonable health, then all of our fantasies will be out the window. The plan is in place: two years to get a new place and dispose of the property we now own. Otherwise, the wheelchair will be first, and the house will be last. Timing is very important. There are many things in our lives at this time that need to be focused on while we're in fairly good health.

DONNA: Now is the time for us to make our plans for change. At this stage of our lives there are lots of adjustments to make. I'm glad I have a partner to make plans with. Together we'll figure it all out. I feel very fortunate. Andy's recent spinal nerve operation and elbow surgery make us aware that time is ticking. And now he has knee problems from old sports injuries that probably will require knee replacements in the future. I've also had a stomach hernia. These are major wake-up calls. The challenge isn't later, it's now. Aging is about the bitter and the better. The bitter is the loss of health, the loss of friends. We've experienced some of that this past year. We realize that it's our job to make the "better" in our future happen. We're in this together. We have a lifetime commitment.

We're very creative people, and we deeply appreciate and encourage that in each other. We bring out the best in each other. We're firm on our commitment. When we were younger, there was always the fear that one of us would bolt, leave, abandon the relationship. Now that we're older, we know that if one of us is sick or handicapped, the other won't leave. We've said to each other, "In sickness, and in health, till death do us part."

Aging is about the bitter and the better.

BETTY AND BILL

Betty is eighty; Bill is eighty-two. They are unmarried and don't live together, but they do spend most of their waking hours, and many of their nights, sharing a happy life. Neither is concerned about what others may think of their relationship.

BETTY: My husband died four years ago. Bill lost his wife two years later. I'd known Bill for many years. He lived right across the street. Bill was a member of a group that would go to breakfast together every Sunday morning after 8:00 mass. One Sunday Bill came up to me after the church service and asked if I'd go with the group to breakfast. As far as I was concerned, this was the beginning of our relationship, but I'm not sure Bill realized it at the time.

BILL: I wasn't really thinking about a relationship when I asked Betty if she'd come with us to breakfast. I wasn't looking for a woman companion at all. After my wife died, I just figured I'd live out my life alone.

BETTY: I wasn't looking for a relationship, either. But we had some mutual friends that kept inviting Bill to dinner, and they'd tell him to pick up Betty on the way over, because they had invited me, too. They kept putting us together, and we got used to it—and we liked it! I never thought I'd find this much happiness at this time of my life—though I told Bill right from the beginning that I didn't want to get married, He didn't, either. It would just complicate things too much with our families. We've made a commitment to each other—Bill bought me a ring—but we don't live together. We see each other every day, and we either go out to dinner or I make supper here at my place. Sometimes Bill stays over night. We live right across the street from each other, so it's easy to get together. We're with each other a lot. Some people may wonder what we're doing together when Bill stays overnight, but it's not their business. Hey, life is short. You have to live your own life and not worry about what other people think.

Some people may wonder what we're doing together when Bill stays overnight, but it's not their business. Hey, life is short. You have to live your own life and not worry about what other people think.

Like when I went to Las Vegas with my daughter a few years ago: She decided to get a tattoo, and I went with her. While we were there, I saw a rose design I thought was pretty, and I had the tattoo guy put a temporary rose on my arm. My neighbors commented on it, and I had fun showing it off. After about a week, the temporary tattoo washed off, but I kept thinking about how much I had enjoyed having it. So, one Saturday morning I went to a tattoo place in town, picked out a lovely rose, and had it tattooed permanently on my wrist. I think a lot of people thought I was crazy getting a tattoo in my seventies, but that was what I wanted to do.

BILL: I know some people tease Betty and say things like "all men want is sex." But that isn't true. There are other things besides sex. Just being close to Betty and touching is really important. I sneak in bed with her a lot. It's been real nice. Betty always has a sparkle in her eye for me. But we just can't sleep in the same bed, because neither of us would get any sleep.

BETTY: We don't actually "sleep" together, because I'm all over the bed—that's how I sleep. I like to cuddle, though, so Bill comes in the bed with me, and we hug and cuddle. I suppose some might think it's funny that old people like us do things like that.

BILL: During the years I was married, I took everything for granted. I didn't tell my wife I loved her as much as I wish I had. I really regret that I just expected her to know I loved her. I realize now how important a relationship is. I tell Betty how much I care all the time, and I really mean it. I call her "precious." We tell each other everything; we don't have any secrets. It's been just great for us both.

We don't actually "sleep" together, because I'm all over the bed—that's how I sleep. I like to cuddle, though, so Bill comes in the bed with me, and we hug and cuddle. I suppose some might think it's funny that old people like us do things like that.

BETTY: We never fight about anything. Actually, we don't even seem to disagree. I don't think we've ever had any big issues to fight about.

BILL: Early in our relationship, if Betty didn't like what I said, she'd just turn away from me and not say anything, not answer me. But that was quite a while ago. I don't remember what the issues may have been. Small things might seem big at the time, but when I stop and look back at a situation clearly, I think, "I love this gal. Why am I upset about small stuff?"

BETTY: Sometimes I wonder why when I'm with Bill I feel like a teenager, but I do! I feel warm and comfortable. My children like Bill and think our relationship is great. They're relieved that they don't have to keep calling me to see if I'm okay. They know I'm happy and busy. It's convenient to have a relationship with someone who lives right across the street.

BILL: I've told my kids that Betty is the light of my life, and they tell me they're very comfortable with my relationship with her. Actually, they seem excited about it. One of my daughters-in-law had some concerns, but everyone else in the family thinks my linking up with Betty is great. We've talked about getting married, but decided not to.

I've told my kids that Betty is the light of my life, and they tell me they're very comfortable with my relationship with her. Actually, they seem excited about it.

BETTY: But we feel married and act married. Except for some health problems, my retirement years really have been my golden years. I had a stroke four years ago. And just when I was getting some of my mobility back, I broke my hip, and I'm still recovering from that.

BILL: I took care of her when she broke her hip. I moved into her house for a couple of weeks. It was a privilege to take care of Betty.

BETTY: The doctor has told me that I've had some heart attacks, too. It might sound strange after hearing about my ailments, but I feel pretty healthy. Bill doesn't have chronic problems like me. He hasn't slowed up much.

BILL: That's true. I water ski, roller blade, and ice skate. Recently, though, my doctor found that my bones have weakened, so now I'm on extra calcium and a prescription pill to strengthen my bones. But that's all. I was warned to avoid doing things where I might fall. Old bones don't heal well. But I still go water skiing, climb ladders, and do a lot of physical stuff. All the work I do daily at the nursery is physical, and I think it's good for me.

My work has always been outdoors and has kept me active. I started my gardening business many years ago. I was a pilot in the army in World War II, and when I came back I took an office job. But I kept looking out the window. I wanted to be outside, so I left that job and went into gardening. At one time I had twenty acres in one location and ten acres in another. Now I'm down to five acres and I manage it myself. My kids and a granddaughter come over once in a while and help, but it's mostly just me. Now it's kind of a hobby—more pleasure than work. It's still a business, but a small one. I don't do it for profit.

We've talked about getting married, but decided not to.... But we feel married and act married.

BETTY: What do we like to do together? We talk to each other a lot. We're easy with each other. We play cards, go to movies once in a while, and visit our friends. We travel some. Our recent trip to Ireland was wonderful, and I want to take Bill to the Black Hills in South Dakota because it's so beautiful there.

I know there are some people who don't want to take on a new relationship when they're older because they worry about the other person dying. We both know that one of us will lose the other sometime in the future. But we're alive now. Why wouldn't people want to be with someone who cares about them? Why wouldn't they want to take a chance on a new relationship?

BILL: When my mother died, my father kept busy with work during the day, but he was all alone at night and on the weekends. When my father remarried, the whole family was thrilled. We hated to see him lonely. I know he loved my mother, but it's important to put your life together after a death. Companionship is very important.

ANN AND JOHN

I met Ann in my water aerobics class. I told her about the interviews I was collecting for my book on late-life relationships, and she invited me to meet her husband, John, that very afternoon. John is seventy-four, and Ann is two years older. When we sat down to talk in their comfortable living room, they held hands. They smiled at one another through our entire conversation as they told the stories of their first marriages and the life they now share.

JOHN: I was an electrical engineer and worked for the same corporation my whole career. I started out as a test engineer and went from there into quality control. I supervised the building of a factory in Singapore and one in Brazil and China. I was eventually elected the national chairman of an aerospace industry quality control committee, and that was the highlight of my career. I've been retired fourteen years now. I had a great career and loved every minute of it. But when I walked away from it, I never looked back. I've really love my retirement: more time to read, more time to spend with friends, more time to be with Ann.

Ann and I met at a series of meetings for a foundation in a very large hospital in our area. We were both financial contributors to the foundation. After spotting Ann at the first meeting, I didn't waste any time asking her out to dinner that night.

ANN: At that meeting, the people around the table introduced themselves and told a bit of their stories. When John spoke, he shared with the group that his wife had been killed instantly in an accident six months earlier. I learned later that she was his second wife and that his first wife had also died suddenly and unexpectedly.

My husband passed away ten years ago. One day he didn't feel well and had a fever. The next day he said he felt better and went to work, though he was coughing. That evening he said he'd sleep in the living room so as not to disturb me

After my husband's death, many times I felt very lonely, particularly on weekends.

with his cough. When I got up in the morning, he was sitting in his chair. I couldn't wake him up. He was gone. It was a terrible shock.

I dealt with the grief of losing my husband by being with other people. I had belonged to a bridge club for thirty years, and now I was the third widow in the group. The first time we met after my husband died we didn't play cards. We talked and cried and laughed and told each other our stories. It was a great comfort. After my husband's death, many times I felt very lonely, particularly on weekends.

JOHN: My first wife and I were high school chums. One night she said she wasn't feeling well and took a sleeping pill to help her get a good rest. I couldn't wake her in the morning. After her death, I remarried, but I was only married two years when my second wife was killed in an accident. I never had a chance to say goodbye to either of them. Both of my wives died with no warning. I wasn't really thinking about looking for a relationship. But then I saw Ann.

ANN: My husband had been gone for ten years, so I think I was more ready for a relationship than John was. I had dated some during those years, but never established a serious relationship. John and I sat together for three days at the foundation meetings. On the last day a formal dinner was scheduled. I had checked out of my hotel because I was driving home after the closing dinner meeting. I had my party clothes in a shopping bag and thought I'd just change in the ladies' restroom. As John and I chatted during that afternoon, he said, "You can come to my room and change." It was strange that when I walked across the street with John I had the feeling that some of the others at the meeting would see me going to his room. I shouldn't have been worried about that at our age, but I felt self-conscious. It wasn't my usual situation. Following the dinner a speaker gave a presentation. During this presentation John reached over and held my hand. I remember thinking, "Wow, this feels good!" No one had held my hand for a long time.

> *After my first wife's death, I remarried, but I was only married two years when my second wife was killed in an accident. I never had a chance to say goodbye to either of them.*

JOHN: I joke that I had her for dinner the first night I met her, and I had her in my bedroom the second night. About a week later I called Ann and invited her to a picnic. We took wine, cheese, and crackers and went down by the river. We had a great time together. It was very romantic.

ANN: Let me give you a little preview to that picnic. After John extended the invitation, I asked my niece if I should bring a casserole. That's a traditional thing for women to do when they visit a man who has lost his wife. And she said, "Heavens, no! Bring a bottle of wine." So we took the wine with us on our picnic, and when we got back to his house after our time by the river, John said he was pretty tired and suggested we take a nap. It ended up being a pretty intense nap, if you know what I mean. We started seeing each other regularly, and I discovered that John was a smart, sensitive, and gentle man. We had a loving and intimate relationship, but I wasn't going to be the one to suggest we get married.

John pulled up in front of a jewelry store.... He said, "Would you like a diamond?" ... I said, "Are you proposing to me?" A quiet "yes" was John's answer. I guess it's hard for some men to get the words out.

One day we were in the car together, and John pulled up in front of a jewelry store and parked. He turned to me and said, "Would you like a diamond?" It was the middle of the day, no moonlight or music or candles, and we were dressed in our blue jeans. I said, "Are you proposing to me?" A quiet "yes" was John's answer. I guess it's hard for some men to get the words out.

We went into the jewelry store, and I was so excited that when the saleslady asked if she could help us I blurted out, "Yes, I just got engaged sitting in that Jeep in front of the store." The saleslady went to the display case, took out a ring, and put in on my finger, and it fit perfectly, so elegant and beautiful. I started feeling a bit strange about it all because John and I really hadn't discussed marriage or anything at all about our future together. Just at that moment the owner of the store came out of the back room with a camera and asked if she could photograph us because it was close to Valentine's Day. And then someone else came out from the back room with a bottle of wine and glasses for everyone. It was a memorable occasion, and we've had grand times together ever since.

Before we were married, John took me on a wonderful trip to Cabo San Lucas. My kids didn't say anything critical when I announced we were going away together, so I don't know if they had negative feelings about me traveling with a man. My daughter is quite religious, and there was time when I wouldn't have thought of doing such a thing. Yet I considered how John and I had both had lived a decent, good life. I didn't feel immoral about doing this. There isn't anything in the Bible about not sleeping together before you're married. Anyway, at this point in my life, I wasn't going to let any negative feelings my kids might have about that bother me.

Before we were married, John took me on a wonderful trip to Cabo San Lucas.... I didn't feel immoral about doing this. There isn't anything in the Bible about not sleeping together before you're married.

So then and now, too, anytime we feel like taking a "roll in the hay" we just go ahead and do it! Both of us can have an orgasm like people in their forties. I never knew that it could be like this after menopause. I never thought that sexual feelings could be so strong in older people. We're married now, and we've just had our second wedding anniversary.

JOHN: I'm deeply in love with Ann. Yes, I was in love with the other women I was married to as well. Ann and I have a hugging, loving relationship. Ours is not a relationship of convenience but of deep love.

ANN: I'm crazy about John. We let each other know we love each other even in the middle of the night. We have a little tapping signal that means "I love you," and we just reach over and touch the other person with that message. And we cuddle a lot. We've found that there are many ways to make love, and we've figured most of them out.

JOHN: I was living in a townhouse when I met Ann, but I hadn't lived there a long time and there was nothing sentimental about the place for me. But I owned a large, beautiful home in Arizona that I really loved. Ann had lived in her home here for over forty years, so we both agreed that her home was perfect for us in the summer and we would live in my home in Arizona in the winter.

We have a little tapping signal that means "I love you," and we just reach over and touch the other person with that message.... There are many ways to make love, and we've figured most of them out.

ANN: I'm a doer, and John is more of a thinker—a reader and scholar. Although I was a secretary all of my work life, I always did a lot of sewing. I still have a small alteration business. When I retired several years ago, I made some cards, passed them around, and set up the business. The business has helped me through my early widowhood. I worked for thirty-one years, so I had a comfortable retirement income. I didn't know John had considerable money when I met him. That didn't matter to me. I fell in love with him, not his assets.

JOHN: We've agreed to keep our assets separate, and we have a written agreement about that. We share the expenses of groceries and other things, but we don't keep track of how much we spend. It's not like that. I probably spend more, but I have more, so it doesn't matter.

I don't have as much energy as I used to have, but I'm taking good care of myself. I've been diabetic for forty-five years. My eyes aren't too good anymore, and my balance isn't very good either. Two months after we were engaged, I woke up with a bad pain in my chest. I knew what was happening, and I did four things immediately: I called 911, took two aspirin, unlocked the front door, and called Ann. I recovered from that heart attack and haven't had a recurrence. I feel pretty good most of the time.

ANN: John has a personal trainer. He exercises, sleeps like a log, eats like a horse—but sensibly. He really takes good care of himself, and I take good care of him.

JOHN: Ann wants to do so much for me that sometimes she makes me feel like a helpless baby. I feel smothered. Once in a while my fuse goes short with all this fawning, and I yell a little bit. We really don't argue, but we came into the relationship with some likes and dislikes and old habits. I guess they can sometimes get in the way.

We really don't argue, but we came into the relationship with some likes and dislikes and old habits. I guess they can sometimes get in the way.

ANN: Yes, I know that I'm often too helpful. I'm a bit compulsive about being neat, and John really isn't. John made soup once, and the mess was all over the kitchen. My comments weren't too nice, and he took a towel and angrily wiped everything up. John is a spot-maker, and I'm a spot-remover. One time we were all dressed up to go out someplace, and he came up to me and said, "Ann, how about checking me for spots?" I guess we've learned to laugh instead of arguing.

If John raises his voice to me, I get hurt. My first husband would yell to get something off his chest, but I hold on to hurt feelings. I resolve things in other ways. I'm not a pushover, but there are other ways to get my point across and be more kind. But in reality, these are small things.

JOHN: When we were dating, I was somewhat reluctant to make any commitments because I wasn't in as good health as Ann. She seems to have as much energy as ever and no serious ailments. I didn't want her to have to be a caregiver or a nurse for me. We both know that declining health is imminent at our age, but we're not letting that reality worry either of us. I tell people who are older and have lost their partner that if they don't attach themselves to another human, especially one that they admire and love, they're missing half of their life.

I tell people who are older and have lost their partner that if they don't attach themselves to another human, especially one that they admire and love, they're missing half of their life.

We both have a lot of friends. Ann has three children—two sons and a daughter—and six grandchildren. I never had any children, but my second wife had eight children, and they're still all good friends of mine. I've got brothers and sisters and many other relatives. They're all overjoyed for us. That has been one of the valuable things in our relationship: that so many people cheer for us. This has been rewarding and greatly appreciated. They were all at our wedding. They loved to see us be this happy.

ANN: John and I have a lot to be thankful for. We're both financially secure; we appreciate our health every day. I thank God every day. And I'm happy that the small stuff isn't as important as it used to be. Our sexual relationship is very important to us, and we take advantage of it every chance we get. We do our separate things during most days. John has his interests and activities, and I have mine. But every day at

5:00 we meet in the living room or on the porch and have one cocktail each. Sometimes we get "distracted," and then dinner waits until later. I've never felt so loving in all my life. Tell that to the young folks, and let them envy it!

SADIE AND MAX

A mutual friend suggested I contact Sadie and Max. When we sat down together to talk, he called her "sweetheart" and she addressed him as "honey." It was obvious they cared deeply for one another. Sadie told me that she was sixty-eight and that Max was an "older man" of eighty. Then she reached over to embrace him. Like other couples in this book, they have chosen, despite the depth of their attachment, to neither marry nor live together.

MAX: I had been married almost fifty years when my wife died. At the unveiling of her tombstone a year after her death, I made a decision that I wanted to be with somebody. I'd had a long marriage and a good life. But my wife was gone, and I was still here, and I was entitled to be happy. I looked around, not for a substitute for my wife but for someone with whom I could share my thoughts and leisure activities. The old saying that everybody needs somebody is true. I tell everybody that if, as you get older, you lose your mate, you should say to yourself, "I did not deal these cards, and

I'm entitled to find somebody else." I had a great, loving wife, but after she was gone I needed someone to share my life with me in a new and different way. A vital part of living is sharing a relationship.

I decided that I would only date women who had been widowed. I chose not to date women who had been divorced, because I just didn't want to hear about bad relationships. People I knew gave me names of women who were available, and I would call and go out to dinner with them. I kept a list of the women and graded them from one to ten. At first I think I was looking for someone physically like my wife of fifty years—tall and thin. But I was immediately attracted to Sadie in spite of her being so physically different from my wife. We just kind of hit it off. She ranked quite high on my rating scale, so I asked her on a second date.

I had a great, loving wife, but after she was gone I needed someone to share my life with me in a new and different way. A vital part of life is sharing a relationship.

SADIE: My husband had only been gone about a year and a half when I went on that first date with Max. I remember that I thought Max was a nice guy but probably not for me. He was quite a bit older and pretty sedate. I thought about fixing him up with one of my friends. But after the fourth date I started to feel differently about him. I was really happy when I was with him. Our physical attraction for each other was amazing and exciting. I was very surprised when that happened. It was unbelievable that two older people like us could have such a range of emotions and be so excited about being together. We had a lot of romance and passion in our relationship. It was like being kids again. I decided not to fix him up with my friend after all.

My mother had had a late-life relationship and love affair, and at the time I never thought they slept together. I just didn't think old people had those kinds of emotions. I realize now that it doesn't make any difference how old you are. We need what we've always needed: physical touch.

MAX: After my wife died, my daughter called me every night. The first night I stayed at Sadie's house, my daughter called as usual, and of course I wasn't there to answer. My daughter became frantic. She called her brothers and sent her husband over to Sadie's house to see if I was there. My car was in her garage and wasn't visible, so my daughter worried even more. My son went over to my house and found my list of women and their ratings. Sadie rated pretty high, so my daughter thought to call her. That ended her search for her father. I really felt awful that I had caused my daughter so much anxiety. However, I just didn't think to call my daughter and make an announcement that I was planning to stay all night with Sadie.

In our first years together Max and I had a very physical relationship.... Now that we've settled into the relationship, we admit we really like to sleep in separate beds.

SADIE: In our first years together Max and I had a very physical relationship. We'd hold hands and touch each other a lot. Now that we've settled into the relationship, we admit we really like to sleep in separate beds. I'm a thrashing machine in my sleep, and Max doesn't move all night. Also, I'm and early-riser and an early-walker, and Max is a late-sleeper.

MAX: We've worked out our intimate times together. Sadie is a great lover. I often stay all night at Sadie's place. We get in bed together until we're ready to go to sleep, and then we each go to sleep in a separate bed. We're not married. I grew up believing that, if you were with someone for a long time and you deeply cared for that person, then ultimately you'd get married and live together. But when I started talking to Sadie about living together, she said something that was very unusual to me. She said, "I love you, and you love me, but we each have our place, our independent activities, and our times with our kids. We live ten minutes apart. If I need you, you're here. If you need me, I'm there. Why live together?" This arrangement really works for us. We've had a relationship for six years now, and this is perfect. I'm amazed that many of my friends have found a partner and set up similar living arrangements. We can be with each other whenever we want, we have our own independence, and we both know we have somebody who really cares to rely on and be with.

SADIE: I never thought much about dating someone who was the same religion. I wasn't very observant and thought it didn't matter. But I want to tell you that the first time I went to the synagogue with Max, it was like a holy experience. It was a beautiful feeling for me. I didn't understand until then that

Many of my friends have found a partner and set up similar living arrangements. We can be with each other whenever we want, we have our own independence, and we both know we have somebody who really cares to rely on and be with.

sharing the same religion did make a difference. It was one more thing that brought us closer.

At first Max had some reservations about introducing me to his family and his close friends. Finally he decided to risk how they might react, and he invited me to a brunch with his daughter and granddaughter. The three of us got along great. That was the real beginning of everything for us. I have three sons, and they really love Max. They had confidence in me making a choice that would make me happy, and that was their primary concern. It wasn't about them; it was all about me. I thought that was very generous of them.

MAX: I admit I was apprehensive at first about Sadie meeting my family. It was very important to me how my children and grandchildren, who were very close to my wife, would accept this relationship. But when they met Sadie it worked out so beautifully I was thrilled. My family loves her; Sadie's family loves me. I couldn't ask for anything more. I feel I'm very blessed.

When I was younger and married, there were all kinds of things to be concerned with, like taking care of the kids, paying bills, building a career, and all those other things that young families deal with that I don't have anymore. Sadie takes care of her family, and I take care of mine. Obviously if there are concerns with my family where Sadie can help in some way she does, and I do the same for her. There are so many things that are typical and normal in a marriage that we don't have in our relationship. The change is in many ways really strange. I was married for almost fifty years, and now I have a whole different kind of relationship. It's like having a second life.

There are so many things that are typical and normal in a marriage that we don't have in our relationship. The change is in many ways really strange.

My life outside of my relationship is rewarding as well. I do a lot of volunteer work in my community and with national organizations. It's not to wear a halo, but it does prove to my grandkids that you can make a difference. I've always believed that one person can make a difference. My purpose isn't to change the world but to do what I can. There are always things to be done. I keep pretty busy.

SADIE: I do a lot of volunteer work, too, but not the same kind. I don't like to be a leader, but I get satisfaction in being the hands-on person. I work at our local food shelf, I drive people to the doctor and other appointments, and I'm ready to participate in whatever needs to be done in my community at any time.

As Max told you, we don't live together, and that has really been a great arrangement for us. We don't have to worry about my money, his money, his kids, my kids—it really works for us. Max is very generous, and he pays whenever we go out together. When we travel, we each pay half. I had suggested that we split the cost of vacations right at the beginning because I like to feel independent. We agree on almost everything—where to go when we plan a trip, what movies to see, where to go for dinner—everything. It's easy: we agree and just enjoy. We spend a good deal of money on travel and such things. We live very well, but I'm getting worried that I'm going to outlive my money. I used to joke about living to one hundred, but you know what? I'm not sure I could afford it!

> *I'm getting worried that I'm going to outlive my money. I used to joke about living to one hundred, but you know what? I'm not sure I could afford it!*

MAX: I guess I'm still okay with money. We're able to afford to take trips, and we enjoy doing that together. We agree so easily on where we want to go and what we want to do. We've been together over six years now, and I don't remember us ever arguing about anything. It's amazing, but we don't have any conflicts or disagreements. I had a wonderful marriage, but we certainly had arguments. Still, we never went to bed mad, and that was important.

SADIE: My marriage wasn't really congenial. I had a very controlling husband, and we did argue. It's so different for Max and me. Max helps me feel calm and good about myself. He has supported me in building a strong self-image. We both figure that when you get to our stage of life, there isn't a whole lot left to argue about. When you don't have to argue about money or kids, what's left? We just want to love each other and be happy. It's strange, but I very often sense the presence of Max's wife and I feel her approval. I had a dream that she and I were in a room together and she said to me, "It's okay, I'm glad you make Max happy, and I'm glad my children love you." In a way it's a blessing on our relationship.

MAX: Sadie and I went to a dinner party recently where there were six couples, and all of them had re-mated, so to speak. All were living separately but were in a committed relationship, and all were extremely happy. Late-life relationships aren't always about marriage or living together. We're not unique in this sense. For many of us living separately is an arrangement that really works. Our relationship is not a replacement or a substitute for the life we had before. It's a different type of situation. Everything is different, but it's beautiful.

We both figure that when you get to our stage of life, there isn't a whole lot left to argue about. When you don't have to argue about money or kids, what's left?

SADIE: Yes, it's beautiful. We know that we're here for one another. Our lives together are very rich. Also, it's wonderful to have a man sitting across the table from me who isn't my son or my friend's husband. Our life now is all about us. In my marriage I cared for my husband, my children, my mother-in-law, and my parents who lived in another state. Now everybody has disappeared. My kids have their own lives and my parents are gone, so it's all about Max. He's the one I concentrate on pleasing—but not taking care of. He's independent and I am, too. We do our own thing, and that's just great. We each pursue our own interests, and we're both interesting to one another. It's all about us now.

MAX: I know my life is going to change. Things won't always be the way they are now. But I don't worry much about sickness or death. When people ask me, "How are you today?" my answer is, "Well, I got out of bed and here I am!" I don't complain anymore. Yes, I ache. I have arthritis. And I have a history of operations from bypass to having a metal plate put in my head. But I think of myself as being in great shape. I'm physically active, I exercise, I'm active in the community. Whatever will be, will be. If Sadie should become physically limited, I'll be there for her, just as I know she would be there for me. We don't talk about or dwell on sickness or death. We put our energy into living every day.

SADIE: Max has had some surgeries, and I've taken care of him for a short time. In a situation that required longer care I would make some provisions for added help and I would want him to do that for me. I wouldn't expect Max to do all the physical work, though I know he'd be there for me. I'd insist on him getting outside help.

We don't talk about or dwell on sickness or death. We put our energy into living every day.

MAX: In some ways I've deliberately ignored the subject of sickness and frailty because you never know what the situation will be. I know we'll be there for each other. Our love wouldn't be any different. We'd each take care of things in a sensible and practical way.

SADIE: Ironically, we'll all be together in the end. Max's wife and my husband are buried very close to each other at the cemetery. That's really serendipity. We're content to know that we'll be together in death as in life.

KATHRYN AND RICHARD

Kathryn is seventy-three, and Richard is sixty-two, eleven years younger. "I guess I've had it both ways," Kathryn explained. "My late husband was twenty-two years older than me." This couple has had their share of ups and downs, changes and challenges. Love doesn't always run smooth, but in this case it runs deep.

RICHARD: We've known each other for twenty-seven years, but we've only been a couple for thirteen of those years. We originally met when I was covering city hall for a community newspaper. I was doing a story on a newly confirmed city official and his deputy, who was Kathryn. I was immediately impressed with her session before the community development committee. I admired her intensity and commitment. After the meeting I happened to ride down on the same elevator with her, and by the time we got to the main floor, I was falling in love with her.

During the months that followed, she became my mentor, colleague, and associate, and we slowly built a friendship. I found that if I wanted the real scoop on what was going on in city hall, and not a political slant, I'd get it from Kathryn. She contributed a lot to what I was writing, and when I started another community paper, she became one of my editorial consultants. She did a lot of editing for me and still does to this day.

KATHRYN: During the time that Richard is describing, I was married to my second husband. My second husband was the psychologist-counselor who helped my daughter and me when my first husband left me for another woman. He was my friend and lover and mentor as well. During that time I maintained my friendship with Richard. Richard was a close and good friend. We didn't see each other very often, but we'd meet for lunch once in a while and talk about what was going on in our personal and professional lives. We'd talk about music, too. Richard knows more about music than any other person I've ever known. Also, we share a sensitivity and appreciation for art. Occasionally we'd meet and go to an art show or a flower show. We shared those events that my husband wasn't interested in attending.

We've known each over for twenty-seven years, but we've only been a couple for thirteen of those years.

My husband passed away after fourteen years of marriage. That was sixteen years ago. The last years of my husband's life he was at home, on oxygen. He was still mentally alert, had a great sense of humor, and we were able to have good conversations. When the end came, he just faded away. He had a good death as deaths go. My mother had died three months previously, and I had been responsible for the care of her, also. During this same period, my son graduated from college, got married, and went into the Peace Corps. I had a killer of a job to handle as well. I ended up having no time or energy to deal with the grief and the fear I was feeling. So I escaped. I went to another city and took a different job.

Shortly before I moved, I went on a picnic with Richard. I recall him saying to me that he would be a great lover if I ever gave him the opportunity. The day I left town I gave Richard a picnic basket full of wonderful food and flowers for another picnic sometime in the future.

RICHARD: Kathryn and I not only had a longstanding friendship, but our sons, who are two years apart in age, knew one another and often spent time together. I knew Kathryn's husband and had the greatest respect and admiration for him. When he was dying, my mother was also in her last days, and during that time Kathryn and I supported each other. We were close friends.

We reached for one another, held hands, and then, yes, we slept together. That was the first time we ever had been intimate, and life sure was different from then on.

It was some time after Kathryn moved away that city hall eliminated the community paper I worked for, and I was forced to take a series of part-time jobs—graphic artwork, freelance editorial work, chauffeuring, security guard—anything for which I had skills.

KATHRYN: We were living in different states and hadn't seen each other for quite some time. I invited Richard to come and visit for his birthday. We went to the theater and the opera, took in a book fair, and planned special meals to celebrate Richard's birthday over the whole weekend.

RICHARD: There was an air of sadness as Sunday evening approached. I was to leave on Monday morning, and we were both feeling a bit down about separating. We reached for one another, held hands, and then, yes, we slept together. That was the first time we ever had been intimate, and life was sure different from then on.

KATHRYN: We arranged to travel to see one another once a month. Then Richard found employment and decided to move in with me in the city where I was living. The job was short term, and our adjustment to living together wasn't without problems, as he was around all day while I was working. We tried moving into a two-bedroom apartment so Richard could keep his books and other things out of the way of our living space, but that didn't work too well either. We did have some wonderful times exploring the city and making new friends. We loved each other, but it was clear that living together wasn't working out. I left my job, and we decided to move back to the city where we both had lived originally.

I bought a home in an area that I had known and always liked, and Richard moved into an apartment in a building where he got a job as the building manager. The process of moving back was stressful, and we separated for a short while. After each of us was settled, we started seeing each other again but not living together.

Our adjustment to living together wasn't without problems.... We separated for a short while.

At this time I was in Alcoholics Anonymous, and I still attend meetings. It had been some time since I had quit drinking and smoking. When we started living together, Richard was still drinking and smoking, and when we moved back and each got our own place, he hadn't given that up. Richard has cerebral palsy, and it wasn't wise for him to take on the job of caretaker in a large building that required so much physical exertion. At the end of a day he was in great pain, and he'd drink to escape from the stress and the pain.

RICHARD: Yes, I was exhausted and in pain at the end of every day, and I drank and took pain pills. One morning I woke up in the hospital in intensive care on a ventilator. I was lucky to survive. After recovering from that extreme experience, I went in psychotherapy, and that's when I became sober. I haven't drank or smoked since. Kathryn was there for me through the whole recovery. She came to see me every day, and we talked on the phone often. I had to move, of course. Fortunately I found public housing and was able to get unemployment. When the unemployment checks ran out, I was accepted for S.S.I. assistance. I live on $825 a month, one third of that immediately goes to rent. I'm not working regularly, but I do things intermittently, like graphic design and dog-sitting.

I thought many times about terminating the relationship, but held on because I observed a continuous process of healing from the blaming and shaming in Richard's youth. His strengths have continued to grow, and his weaknesses have gradually disappeared.

KATHRYN: Those months before things normalized for Richard were very stressful. I thought many times about terminating the relationship, but held on because I observed a continuous process of healing from the blaming and shaming in Richard's youth. His strengths have continued to grow, and his weaknesses have gradually disappeared.

RICHARD: That we've been in Alcoholics Anonymous together has been tremendously important. It has brought us very close. We give each other a great deal of mutual support. Another significant thing in our relationship was that we adopted a toy poodle named Butch. I'd take care of Butch when Kathryn traveled for work, and when we went camping we'd always take Butch along. The dog is no longer alive, but while we had him he was a focal point, a real adhesive in our relationship. We both love dogs.

KATHRYN: Another thing that brought us closer together is Richard's relationship with my relatives. My brother is eighty-one, and we all love to spend time together. My sister is eighty-four and an absolute joy to be around. We often take her on vacations with us.

Until very recently, I was employed by a local university. My work involved creating a late-life learning network for older people and was very rewarding. That job has ended, and now I'm drawing down my 401k. They will be used up in three years. I'm looking around for something interesting and stimulating that can give me an additional income.

These past months I've felt that I'm transitioning into a different phase of my life. In the past, I've been so busy and involved in my work that I haven't spent as much time as I'd like with Richard. This may sound silly, but I get hungry for him. I miss the intimacy and time alone with Richard when I'm committed to participating in conferences and launching new projects. I'm ready to change my pace.

These past months I've felt that I'm transitioning into a different phase of my life. I miss the intimacy and time alone with Richard when I'm committed to participating in conferences and launching new projects. I'm ready to change my pace.

Knowing my job was going to end, I've been saying things to Richard like, "Maybe I'll move to Seattle," "It would be nice to move to Cape Cod," or "There's a new co-housing project being created in upstate New York that really intrigues me." I now realize that my saying these things has been threatening to Richard. Only in the last few months have I understood this, and I've been apologetic and regretful. I now see how important it is for Richard to know that my love is unconditional. I've recently thought a lot about what would happen to us if I moved to a different city and Richard didn't choose to move. It's ridiculous for me to play that game any-more. I've stopped talking about leaving, and I've stopped thinking about moving elsewhere in the country.

Since my job terminated, our relationship has really changed. We've grown into a different stage of our life togeth-er. Richard and I have talked about changing our living arrangements, possibly getting a house with an adjacent apart-ment so that Richard could have his space and I'd have mine and yet we could more easily come together. We've also dis-cussed such options as co-housing and cooperative housing. I'm confident we'll find something that feels right to us both.

These days I feel a new stability in our relationship. My sense of where we're at is more comforting and relaxed, yet also more intense— in good ways. There's more accommodation on both our parts, and it makes a great difference.

Richard has always had to deal with depression. It's a chemical thing. It used to cause problems in our relationship, but I understand it better now, and he does, too. He's learned to keep his low periods shorter, and I no longer overreact when he goes into a down period. He's able to come back to a place of stability, and I honor that. We have a new depth in our relationship. I know I've changed in some ways as well.

RICHARD: I think Kathryn has learned patience with my down times. And I also think that her patience and under-standing have helped them to become less frequent and not as low. We both know now when we need to break and be sepa-rate for a short while. Her patience helps me get back on track sooner. These days I feel a new stability in our relationship. My sense of where we're at is more comforting and relaxed, yet also more intense—in good ways. There's more accommodation on both our parts, and it makes a great difference.

I value, beyond measure, our intimacy. We're totally compatible in our interests, particularly our interest in the arts. Just yesterday we were planning what dance events, concerts, and art exhibits we wanted to attend. I write a good deal of poetry, but I don't consider a poem finished until Kathryn puts her expertise and sensitivity into it. She's my best editor. It's so rich what we share. I cherish this richness, even in everyday things. We love to cook together, and we enjoy being outdoors—walking and hiking. When Kathryn comes home from traveling, I welcome her with a verse. This is one from when she came back from a conference a few days ago:

> Commingle a rose with a poem.
> Petals of verse and love become one.

KATHRYN: Whenever Richard welcomes me home with something like that, I treasure it. How many people do you know who have someone who loves them and writes poetry for them? I feel so lucky. Up until now my life has been lived by the calendar. I've thrived on being overbooked. But since I left my job, we have more time for the small things. Strolling slowly through an art gallery, for instance. We take time to discuss the paintings and our different opinions about which piece we like best and why. It's all really very rich.

I'm more myself than the self that other people expect me to be. Age has brought me freedom.

At this time of my life, I'm more myself than the self that other people expect me to be. Age has brought me freedom. Ironically, my expanding appreciation for Richard has actually added to my sense of freedom. In my slowing-down I've discovered nuances not only of myself but of our relationship. New dimensions of living are opening up for me. Embracing our relationship more honestly has given me more freedom. That was a surprise. Now I'm beginning to resent the many volunteer obligations I've taken on that keep me from being with Richard.

Richard is romantic. Everything about our intimate relations is wonderful. Richard is the world's best lover. I've never had a physical relationship with a man that was truly satisfying, in which there wasn't some female artifice to make the man feel good. I didn't know what sexual relations were really about. With Richard, I find ecstasy. Now that's pretty great, isn't it?

Because of financial issues and the fact that we both need our own space, we've decided not to marry. We spend weekends together and time during the week as well. We live about ten minutes away from each other. Most nights when we're not together, we talk on the phone. We sort of tuck each other in by phone.

I've never had a physical relationship with a man that was truly satisfying, in which there wasn't some female artifice to make the man feel good. With Richard, I find ecstasy.... Now that's pretty great, isn't it?

RICHARD: For lack of a better term, I consider us as being married. What I want most from Kathryn is not to be cared for but to be cared about. We have made a commitment for life to each other. I want Kathryn to be the last woman in my life, and I want her to know that.

LAURA AND ROBERT

Robert is seventy-eight. He teaches one day a week at a local college, where he once was a full-time member of the faculty. His wife died eight years ago. Robert's five children, seventeen grandchildren, and eight great-grandchildren still live nearby, so his house is often full of family of all ages. Laura is seventy-five, has three grown children, and has been divorced for thirty-eight years. She's had a varied career: writing, speaking, and often teaching. Though she has had long-term relationships with a few men in the many years since her divorce, she has never settled down with any of them. "I guess it absolutely had to be the right guy for me if I was going to have a lasting relationship," she said. Laura and Robert have been a couple for five years, but they've known each other for much longer.

LAURA: I've known Robert for over fifty years. His wife and I had babies around the same time, so we were both house-bound at the same time. Our husbands were just starting their first jobs out of college. I was asked to join a small book discussion group of young mothers, and that's where I met Robert's wife. One night a month, while our husbands baby-sat the children, we met for intellectual stimulation. After a few years, six of us invited our husbands to play cards one evening, and that established a bridge club that met month-ly for several years. That's how I first knew Robert.

ROBERT: Several years later, during the late 1960s, when many kids were having trouble in school, two of my sons and Laura's daughter left the public school system and entered into what were then some early experiments in community-based education and have since developed into the alternative school movement. Then Laura moved out of town sometime in the mid-1970s, and our fam-ilies drifted apart.

Robert said, "Hey, call me when you come visit again, and we'll have lunch and talk about old times." I took him up on that offer. Our lunch lasted almost six hours, and then it was time for dinner!

LAURA: I took a job in the East and lived there for thirteen years, then moved west for another thirteen. Six years ago Robert and I ran into each other on one of my visits back to my old hometown. Robert said, "Hey, call me when you come visit again, and we'll have lunch and talk about old times." I took him up on that offer. Our lunch lasted almost six hours, and then it was time for dinner! We've been together for almost five years now. The first year and a half was a long-distance relationship. I didn't decide to move back until I was sure that building a life together was what I wanted.

ROBERT: I lived alone for over a year after my wife died. Well, almost alone—I did have my dog for company. When

Laura and I met for lunch, it felt so comfortable talking about the many things we had in common and catching up on old friends. I really didn't think I was looking for a permanent relationship, but Laura was interesting and cute and funny. I enjoyed the time with her that day and hoped we'd stay in touch.

LAURA: Robert did stay in touch. He called and wrote to me, and then we started sending e-mail to each other. He suggested he'd like to come to visit for a weekend so I could show him around the city I lived in. I don't think we did much sightseeing. We were in bed most of the time!

ROBERT: Now our sex life isn't as energetic or as active as those first days, but our physical relationship is very satisfying. We may not have sex the same way as when we were younger, but we have good sex, satisfying and enjoyable, with tender intimacy, and we enjoy each other's body a great deal. We have mutual oral sex, which gives me great pleasure, and Laura tells me that it's pleasurable for her as well. We both sleep nude, and we cuddle when we go to bed and when we wake up in the early morning. A night rarely goes by without touching and cuddling.

We may not have sex the same way as when we were younger, but we have good sex, satisfying and enjoyable, with tender intimacy, and we enjoy each other's body a great deal.

LAURA: For many months we both assumed that we'd keep our long-distance romance going. It was fun, exciting, and romantic. We didn't discuss a permanent future together, but we did plan some interesting travel together and scheduled several future visits to one another. But I sensed very quickly that Robert didn't want a transient relationship. I knew that when he was back home he wasn't seeing other women or accepting their invitations to come over for dinner. At first, that actually scared me.

Many years earlier, my husband had left me abruptly for another woman, and I never trusted any relationship I was in afterward. I had to learn to trust before I could make a commitment. I know I tested Robert many ways during our first year together, maybe even longer. It wasn't anything he said or did; it was my inability to trust. I knew the problem was mine, and I seriously worked on it. Robert didn't disappear, didn't back out, didn't waiver. He wanted the relationship, and he had the maturity and understanding to hang on.

Many years earlier, my husband had left me abruptly for another woman, and I never trusted any relationship I was in afterward. I had to learn to trust before I could make a commitment.

ROBERT: After we had been seeing each other for well over a year, Laura and I had a conversation about how foolish it seemed for two people in their seventies who cared a great deal about each other to be living a couple of thousand miles apart. There wasn't any question that if one of us moved it would be Laura. My whole family still lived here, and Laura's daughter, her cousins, and many old friends were here, too. Laura still had roots in this part of the country in spite of having moved away over twenty-five years earlier.

LAURA: My dilemma was where to settle if I moved. Robert's house didn't have any space for my antique furniture, or empty closets for my clothes, or storage room for the rest of my stuff. I needed space for a home office, too. Our compromise was interesting. I bought a small condominium five minutes drive from Robert's place, and we worked out a way to live together in two houses. Every week we choose what days and nights we'll pack up the milk, the bread, and the dog and move temporarily into the other house for a few days. If one of us ever feels the need to be alone, we have a quiet retreat available at the other house. It works fine for us, at least for now.

ROBERT: In addition to the housing arrangement, other things work for us as well. We share a love and tenderness for each other, and we're compatible in our interests and our politics. I have strong political convictions, and I'm happy that Laura shares a similar viewpoint. People often ask if and when we're going to get married. We've talked about it, but I don't think that we will. Our situation now is very comfortable and with things as they are, neither of us is required to face the technical and material issues that a marriage would create. I believe we both get from the relationship the things we want and need. I feel completely committed, and I think Laura feels the same way.

When people ask me when we're going to get married, I jokingly say, "We don't have to, I'm not pregnant." Then the question doesn't come up again.

LAURA: When people ask me when we're going to get married, I jokingly say, "We don't have to, I'm not pregnant." Then the question doesn't come up again. I feel committed to Robert in a married sense. I think if Robert wanted to get married and he kept saying to me, "Let's think about getting married," then I might seriously think about it. But it isn't on his priority list. He does everything to show his commitment to the relationship, so there's no pressure from either of us to get married and deal with all the details of wills and estate and all that. Now, after I've said all that, I must confess that sometimes I feel I would like to get married. I trust the relationship the way it is, but I occasionally wonder if there would be a possibility of us growing together in a different way, in a deeper way, if we married.

I get a great deal from our relationship the way it is. The comfort of the consistency is something that I value and enjoy. I trust he's there for me. I've spent years and years living with the fear that I was going to be abandoned. I suffered with that fear as a child, and my husband literally did abandon me and our three children. Then during the many years after my divorce when I was alone I would get into relationships in which I consciously or unconsciously felt I was going to be left, and indeed a number of those relationships terminated with my being abandoned.

I went into the relationship with Robert with those same fears, and I gave him some difficult times. I quickly saw I was acting on old patterns and that I would probably sabotage the relationship, so I sought out counseling. I worked hard to understand and change my old patterns. It was kind of a miracle when I was able to gain new insights and change my behavior. One day while I was in therapy that feeling of fear and certainty that I would be left vanished and never returned. It was truly a miracle that allowed me to love without fear. Those old fears of abandonment no longer have anything to do with my life.

I don't want to turn something that's done by us with consent every day into some kind of compulsory contract.
I renew my commitment to our relationship voluntarily every day.

ROBERT: Our relationship is great, but we probably won't get married. One reason I'd rather not marry is that I don't want to turn something that's done by us with consent every day into some kind of compulsory contract. I renew my commitment to our relationship voluntarily every day. And, too, if we married, we'd have to spend an enormous amount of time and energy talking about money and inheritance and things like that because of our two families. It's just something I don't want to have to do, but that's less important than that our relationship is at all times voluntary and chosen each day. Marriage might change this. Marriage can be like being "stuck." As things are now, I re-commit to the relationship every day, and that keeps it lively and exciting for me.

LAURA: One thing in our relationship that impresses me is that Robert always pays his bills on time. He has no major debts and is quite generous with his money. I pay my bills on time, too, and I always watch and respect my bank balance. We have similar habits of responsibility.

We've never formally worked out a financial agreement. We each pay our own bills for our separate households. Robert voluntarily pays for our vacations. He also covers the bigger share of the groceries and our meals we eat out. Robert can more easily pay for the larger portion of our expenses, and he's very willing to do so. I give money to my children and grandchildren when they need help, and Robert does the same for his family. It all works out agreeably.

We've never formally worked out a financial agreement. We each pay our own bills for our separate households.... It all works out agreeably.

ROBERT: Laura has one habit that I have a hard time with and that I don't really understand: she can't throw anything away. No matter how full her closets get, no matter how many boxes of shoes and purses she has, she still goes shopping and she doesn't get rid of anything. She just can't resist a bargain, and when something is marked down fifty percent, plus there's an extra twenty percent off for "senior day," Laura buys it even if she doesn't need it.

LAURA: In my defense I want to say that I read recently in a magazine article that "retail therapy"—that's shopping—relieves stress for many women. I guess I'm one of those.

ROBERT: Moving off this subject (before I get into trouble) and looking at another issue ... neither of us is in perfect health. I'm doing okay, but my energy has changed considerably. I'm disappointed that I can't take long walks anymore. I'm out of breath going up the smallest hill. It's irritating, stressful, and limiting not to be able to do what I did so easily five years ago. Recently I've had heart valve replacement surgery, and I also have a pacemaker. I suspect that at some point one of us will become a caregiver for the other. We would have been wise to discuss this subject during the early part of our relationship, but we didn't, although we both know that as we get older we're likely to have more physical limitations and problems and need special care. It's hard, however, to talk about "what if."

I suspect that at some point one of us will become a caregiver for the other. We would have been wise to discuss this subject during the early part of our relationship, but we didn't, although we both know that as we get older we're likely to have more physical limitations and problems and need special care. It's hard, however, to talk about "what if."

LAURA: I feel I have been a caregiver already. I was a caregiver during the months before Robert's surgery when he was quite limited in his activities and after the surgery as well. I didn't travel for my work or to visit my children and grandchildren while I felt Robert needed my help. During a period of about six or seven weeks, when Robert was the most needing of care, I learned a lesson about being a caregiver that I knew intellectually but had never experienced. I got very worn out physically and somewhat angry at being totally limited by Robert's needs. I learned the hard way what I believe needs to be the caregiver's mantra: "Take care of yourself so you can take care of others."

ROBERT: I expect it's some comfort to Laura that I was a caregiver for my wife for a long period of time and for my mother-in-law who lived with us as well. I can certainly see myself in the role of caregiver. It's really a form of denial not to think and talk about the possibility of one or the other being faced with caregiving responsibilities. But the need is unknown at this time, and the arrangements to be made depend on so many variables.

LAURA: Several years ago I purchased a long-term care policy, so I'll have that financial assistance available, and that's some comfort. Robert has considerable financial security, so he can comfortably arrange to stay in his home if he would need a great deal of care. I know that if I were the one needing care that Robert would take on that responsibility. But he's considerably older now than when he put in day and night hours caring for both his wife and mother-in-law, and he's not in as good health as during that time. I'm confident that Robert would spend time with me and take care of me as best he could and that he'd hire people to come in to do some of the care. If nothing else, he'd read poetry to me, or we'd play gin rummy while some hired helper would do what needed to be done.

I learned the hard way what I believe needs to be the caregiver's mantra: "Take care of yourself so you can take care of others."

Meanwhile, at this time we're both in pretty stable health. We've recently taken a trip to Europe and have another trip planned for New York. We've slowed our pace somewhat, and we're okay with that. We no longer plan so many activities in one day that we end up exhausted. Robert does best when he takes a nap in the afternoon.

ROBERT: We're pretty realistic about the changes in our energy, so we ration it carefully. We exercise regularly at the gym, and Laura goes to a water aerobics class. We're careful to eat well. Laura is a big salad maker, and I've learned to enjoy that. At this time we seem to have an abundance of good days. I'm still teaching one day a week at a local college, and Laura writes articles and occasionally takes on writing a book. I think we have a good balance of leisure and activity. I often give Laura roses, and I enjoy buying her jewelry. She's got a very special ring from me on the third finger of her left hand. We have everything we need, and, thankfully, we have each other.

ABOUT THE AUTHOR

Connie Goldman is an award-winning independent public radio producer, author, and public speaker, formerly on the staff of National Public Radio. She is the author of five books and is a recipient of the Senior Award from the American Society on Aging. She lives near the Twin Cities of Minneapolis and Saint Paul, Minnesota.